CONCEPTS IN
CANADIAN
NURSING

CONCEPTS IN CANADIAN NURSING

Janet Ross Kerr, R.N., Ph.D.

Professor, Faculty of Nursing
University of Alberta
Edmonton, Alberta

Jannetta MacPhail, M.S.N., Ph.D., F.A.A.N., LL.D. (Honorary)

Professor Emeritus, Faculty of Nursing
University of Alberta
Edmonton, Alberta

 Mosby

St. Louis Baltimore Boston Carlsbad Chicago Naples New York Philadelphia Portland
London Madrid Mexico City Singapore Sydney Tokyo Toronto Wiesbaden

Publisher: Nancy L. Coon
Executive Editor: N. Darlene Como
Project Manager: Mark Spann
Production Editor: Holly Roseman
Electronic Production Coordinator: Wendy Bellm
Designer: Judith J. Lang
Manufacturing Manager: Tony McAllister

Printed in the United States of America
Composition by Mosby Electronic Production
Printing/binding by Malloy

Mosby-Year Book, Inc.
11830 Westline Industrial Drive
St. Louis, Missouri 63146

Library of Congress Cataloging in Publication Data
Kerr, Janet C., 1940-
    Concepts in Canadian nursing / Janet Ross Kerr, Jannetta MacPhail.
      p. cm.
    Includes bibliographical references and index.
    ISBN 0-8016-8107-3
    1. Nursing—Canada.   I. MacPhail, Jannetta.   II. Title.
    [DNLM: 1. Nursing—Canada.   WY 300 DC2 K4c 1996]
RT6.A1K47   1996
610.73'0971—dc20
DNLM/DLC
for Library of Congress   95-36946
                                    CIP

95 96 97 98 99 / 9 8 7 6 5 4 3 2 1

PREFACE

This book is an attempt to bring the special issues and concerns of nursing in Canada to the reader in a succinct, readable, and meaningful form. It is intended primarily for students in nursing programs, although nurses in practice also may find it useful as a resource book. Clinical issues are addressed alongside broader professional issues. We thus hope that this book will be useful to the Canadian reader as a companion volume to the large clinical textbooks in which the context is predominantly that of nursing in the United States. Because health is a highly political concept in both the value of health to the society and how much the society is willing to risk to promote and maintain the health of people, different countries manage health differently. These differences may be extensive in some cases and subtle in others. Nevertheless, health is framed by the nature of a people and the context in which they live. These reasons alone require that issues in nursing and health are thoroughly examined from the standpoint of Canadian society.

Rapid change in the modern world is reflected in health and in nursing as an important component of health care. In fact, the sheer volume of change in the past 5 years, even within the last year, is difficult to track, let alone address. Perhaps we have attemped the impossible in documenting trends and issues in nursing and in discussing their relevance to the field. However, we believe nurses must understand how the profession has evolved in Canada and the complex issues nurses face as they enter professional practice. Nurses of the future must have the background to assume leadership roles in health care and to shape the character of the profession as it works to improve the service provided to consumers. Nurses also must be prepared to enter the policy arena to give nursing a strong voice as the health-care system of the future unfolds. We hope that the quality of nursing will be increased through the understanding and competence gained by those who are committed to addressing the many challenges that lie ahead.

Janet Ross Kerr
Jannetta MacPhail

ACKNOWLEDGEMENTS

The following authors have contributed chapters to this book, and we are grateful for the important contributions they have made to the substance and quality of the content:

Margaret J. Harrison, R.N., Ph.D.
Professor, Faculty of Nursing
The University of Alberta
Edmonton, Alberta

Anita Molzahn, R.N., Ph.D.
Associate Professor and Director, School of Nursing
The University of Victoria
Victoria, British Columbia

Linda Reutter, R.N., Ph.D.
Associate Professor, Faculty of Nursing
The University of Alberta
Edmonton, Alberta

CONTENTS

CONCEPTS IN CANADIAN NURSING

NURSING IN CANADA: HISTORICAL OVERVIEW

JANET ROSS KERR

France laid claim to vast territory along the St. Lawrence River as a result of voyages of Jacques Cartier, including his 1535 landing on Newfoundland, where he established a small settlement from which to explore the continent further. In 1608, Samuel de Champlain selected Quebec as the site for the first permanent settlement along the St. Lawrence River because of its suitability as a centre for the fur trade. The settlement of New France parallels the development of nursing because a hospital and health-care system developed before the fur-trading community expanded to include settlers who were not directly involved in the fur trade. Providing education, health care, and social welfare for the large indigenous population was seen as an important goal from the outset by the missionaries who accompanied the fur traders to the new land. The French authorities concurred with these religious goals, but they also may have seen the importance of converting the native peoples as a way of ensuring their cooperation with those involved with the burgeoning and lucrative fur trade. Not all of the native peoples were friendly, and the French settlers had to endure hostile conflicts with some tribes over a long time, as the native peoples resented the intrusion of the European fur traders and settlers.

■ The Origins of Nursing in New France

Nursing in Canada and nursing in Britain differed markedly during the seventeenth and eighteenth centuries. Nursing in Britain fell into disrepute after Henry VIII renounced the Catholic Church and ejected the Catholic nursing sisterhoods from the large London hospitals. These nurses were replaced by those of the "Sairey Gamp" type satirized by Dickens. Many descriptions of uncaring and incompetent staff who were more concerned with their own pleasure than the comfort of patients are available (Gibbon and Mathewson, 1947). However, these conditions did not appear to any extent in Canada because the settlements in Quebec developed as colonies of France from the outset and included the system of French nursing by nuns who were highly committed to their work and under whom the quality of care was excellent. Young women of good character were recruited to nursing in France under the auspices of the Catholic Church. As Gibbon and Mathewson have noted:

> If the settlements along the St. Lawrence River had been colonized in the seventeenth century by the English instead of by the French, the history of nursing in Canada might have been very different. Fate, however, decided in favour of the French, and that was fortunate both for the Huron and Algonquin Indians and for the white pioneers, since in the wake of the fur traders and coureurs de bois, came the Augustinian Hospitallers or Nursing sisters of Dieppe to Quebec and the St. Joseph Hospitallers of La Fleche to Montreal on their missions of healing and of mercy–missions which had no counterpart in the colonizing efforts of the Protestant English in North America (1947, p. 1).

The system of health-care was firmly established by the time of the conflict between the English and the French on the Plains of Abraham, after which the area became a colony of England. The fact that the vast majority of inhabitants of the colony continued to be French, as well as the factor of the geographic separation from England, no doubt served to ensure continuation of French standards and control in the existing system.

The Augustinian Sisters at Quebec

The first nurses to arrive on the shores of Quebec were three Augustinian nuns from Dieppe who came in August of 1639 after a voyage of 3 months' duration. Upon arrival, they found themselves in the midst of an epidemic, and they were thrown into their work from the outset. They had been accompanied on the voyage by three Ursuline sisters who were going to Quebec as well; their mission was to establish a school to provide education to the native children. However, the Ursulines "found themselves nursing instead of teaching" (Millman, 1965, p. 424) as they assisted the Augustinian sisters in caring for the sick until the epidemic that met them at their arrival had subsided. Only after some time could they focus on their mission of establishing a school. As the settlement increased in size and their work increased, the nuns augmented their ranks by calling for new recruits from Dieppe. Epidemics of typhus, smallpox, and other infectious diseases occurred regularly, and the death toll was high among those who became ill. Many of the sisters also died as a result of exposure to disease. In the smallpox epidemic of 1703, more than a quarter of the nuns died (Gibbon and

Mathewson, 1947). Eventually with the growth of the settlement, they were able to find young women for their nursing order, and they no longer needed to solicit new recruits from France.

Jeanne Mance

Although most of the nurses who came to New France were members of religious orders, one notable exception was Jeanne Mance. She often has been called Canada's most famous nurse, and indeed the Canadian Nurses Association (CNA) named its highest award in her honour. The Jeanne Mance award is given to those who have made distinguished contributions to Canadian nursing. In France, Jeanne Mance had regularly read the *Jesuit Relations*, annual accounts of life and conditions in New France written by the Jesuit priests and intended to raise public awareness of the needs of the colony and to raise funds for its support. Fund raising was an important ongoing process because the French colony was not allowed to trade with the English colonies in North America. Jeanne Mance believed that she had been called to serve in New France and was asked by a wealthy benefactor to establish a hospital at Montreal. She prepared herself for nursing and sailed for Quebec in the summer of 1641 with 3 women and 40 men under the leadership of Paul de Chomédy, Sieur de Maisonneuve (CNA, 1968). The party arrived too late in the summer to be able to make the journey upriver to Montreal and to construct living quarters before the onset of winter. Those at Quebec suspected that the party intended to establish another settlement and fur-trading centre along the St. Lawrence, undoubtedly because they viewed it as a competitive settlement: "Every means was used to persuade the adventurers to abandon their project" (Parkman, 1897, p. 296). However, those bound for Montreal remained steadfast and arrived at the site of the future city of Montreal on May 17, 1642, from which point they proceeded to establish their settlement. Although the hospital was one of the first buildings to be constructed on the site, some among the group had misgivings:

> It is true that the hospital was not wanted as no one was sick at Ville Marie and one or two chambers would have sufficed for every prospective necessity, but it will be remembered that the colony had been established in order that a hospital might be built . . . Instead then of tilling the land to supply their own pressing needs, all labourers of the settlement were set at this pious though superfluous task (Parkman, 1897, p. 362).

All of the settlers were committed to converting the natives to Christianity, and the hospital was seen as an important part of this goal. Before long, the new hospital was busy. At the outset Mlle Mance cared for settlers wounded by attacks of the Iroquois, but she had her hands full nursing both the settlers and the natives in her hospital. Jeanne Mance was considered one of the founders of the city of Montreal, and she assisted Maisonneuve with keeping the accounts of the colony.

She made three fund-raising trips back to France during her lifetime. During her final visit in 1659, she arranged for the Sisters of St. Joseph to come to assist her because, nearing the end of her career, she needed to arrange for continuation of her work. When she died in 1673, she was "universally respected and beloved by the Colony which she had helped found" (Gibbon and Mathewson, 1947, p. 30).

The Grey Nuns

The Sisters of Charity of Montreal, more commonly known as the Grey Nuns, are a uniquely Canadian order founded on December 31, 1737 by Mme Marguerite d'Youville about a century after the arrival of the first nurses at Quebec. Mme d'Youville was a widow and the niece of the French Canadian explorer La Vérendrye when she set about with a band of women to do good work for those in need in the community. The order she founded was also the first noncloistered order to be founded in Canada, and the Grey Nuns thus were able to do home visiting, nursing patients in their homes. This had never been done in the colony before, and at first some mistrusted their work. The Grey Nuns were obliged to make their visits in pairs for protection. The name they maintain proudly to this day, the Grey Nuns, arose from misunderstanding and false rumours, as they were called "les soeurs grises" or the tippling nuns. The Grey Nuns continued their home visiting and proved their value to the community, where they became trusted and respected. The name that they were given in derision became a mark of honour.

In 1745 after a fire destroyed their house, they moved from place to place to carry on their work. When the owners of the General Hospital offered the hospital to Mme d'Youville under a charter, the nuns made it the centre of their operations. The Grey Nuns were enterprising and ran many businesses to pay their debts. They made military garments and tents and ran a brewery, a tobacco plant, and a freight and cartage business. Those whose health was restored as a result of the sisters' efforts were asked to make a contribution in service to assist in their charitable work. When war broke out between the French and the English in 1756, they designated a section of the hospital, known as the Ward of the English, to care for wounded English soldiers. They provided care to anyone in need, and when they gave refuge to escaped English soldiers fleeing from the Indians, "one of these English showed his gratitude, in 1760, by saving the hospital from the artillery fire of the army of invasion" (Gibbon and Mathewson, 1947, p. 48).

■ Health During the Transition to British Rule

After the war years between 1756 and 1763, the nursing sisters, who were thoroughly Canadian by now and had rejected offers to return to France, were plunged into conditions of almost abject poverty. There were no longer funds from France to support activities of the colony, and their wealthy benefactors had returned to

France at the termination of French rule in the colony. Because of the respect the British soldiers held for the sisters, the Prime Minister of Great Britain, William Pitt, communicated with the Duchesse d'Aiguillon, niece of the woman through whose generosity the Hôtel Dieu at Quebec had been founded, and conveyed the message that "our officers, who are very strong in their praises of the charitable care of our sick and wounded by these nuns, have paid them every attention required by piety and misfortune" (Gibbon and Mathewson, 1947, p. 52). Evidence also shows that the British provided some financial assistance to the sisters: "By instruction of Pitt, General Murray relieved the Hôtel Dieu of a debt of taxes to the extent of 3,389 livres, which had reverted to the British at the change of the regime, and also paid £808 for rent of lodgings to the troops, and £3,085 for the use of furniture, laundry and utensils of the hospital" (Gibbon and Mathewson, 1947, p. 52-53). The nuns had established a reputation for a warm and human approach and superb care when patients from both sides of the battle were brought to the Hôtel Dieu during the American War of Independence of 1775 and 1776. The fact that a number of hospitals had been built in various settlements by the time French rule ended was fortuitous, for the health system they had founded was well established and would continue. All of the nursing orders in Canada placed a high value on the preservation of human life and nourishment of the spirit through religious beliefs and practices, and these remained distinguishing features of their mission.

■ Immigration and Infectious Diseases

Because the English were outnumbered by the French, in making the transition to British rule the British encouraged immigration of English-speaking settlers. Although the British originally anticipated that English settlers would come to Canada in large numbers, this did not occur. The Quebec Act of 1774 was important in that it restored many of the rights that French Canadians had held before the hostilities, and it helped retain the support of the French during the War of Independence. United Empire Loyalists, those in the 13 colonies who remained loyal to Britain during the War of Independence, were given refuge and land in Canada, and the number who moved north eventually totalled 50,000. The poverty resulting from the effect of the Napoleonic Wars on trade in the British Isles led many to move to Canada, where they hoped they would have a better life. Many of the new immigrants were poorly nourished and in somewhat less than robust health when they stepped aboard the disease-infested ships that would take them to their new land. The death toll on the ships was high, and the immigrants carried contagious diseases to the settlements in Canada. Although the United Empire Loyalists did not have to contend with the perils of ocean travel on ships that were rife with pestilence and at first enjoyed better health than the immigrants, they nevertheless succumbed to infections that were brought ashore by the immigrants from Britain.

Diseases such as smallpox, typhus, cholera, typhoid, and trachoma were brought to Canada by immigrants and travelers, and epidemics were continuous. In 1832, a cholera epidemic wiped out one quarter of the population of Montreal, a total of 4000 people (Gibbon and Mathewson, 1947).

Hospitals were established during this time as waves of successive epidemics swept the country. Isolating victims of epidemics from the healthy community and providing good nursing care to them was the best that could be done. In newly established English settlements where there were no French-Canadian nursing orders, the quality of nursing was considerably lower and had more in common with standards in British hospitals. However, in areas of the country served by the French-Canadian nursing orders, the central characteristics of humane and competent nursing service were maintained. These would serve as excellent models for areas where the population was composed mainly of British settlers and where, in some of the new health institutions, nursing was sadly wanting.

■ The Impact of Florence Nightingale's Reforms on Nursing in Canada

Florence Nightingale saw the problems in nursing in Britain and decided that her life's work would be to nurse the sick. She came from a background of wealth and social position, and against strong opposition from her family, she prepared herself for nursing. After this she secured a position as a matron in a London hospital. She then was able to secure the approval of the British government for a mission to provide nursing care to wounded British soldiers during the Crimean War, and she ventured to the battlefield with her party of 38 carefully selected nurses. Her amazing feat in restoring the health of large numbers of wounded British soldiers by improving sanitation and standards of cleanliness and by providing excellent care to those who were ill resounded throughout the world. As a consequence, nursing became a suitable occupation for women, who previously had not been allowed to engage in gainful work outside the home. Schools of nursing were established in North America on the model of the Nightingale school that she established in 1860 after her triumphant return from the Crimea. The School of Nursing she established in association with St. Thomas' Hospital in London was made possible by the proceeds from the Nightingale Fund, a fund comprising donations from those in Britain and around the world who had appreciated her work with wounded soldiers in the Crimea. Nightingale had a profound influence on nursing internationally and, as a result, nursing became a respectable occupation for secular women of good character. The first school of nursing founded on the Nightingale model in Canada was St. Catharine's Training School, established on June 10, 1874, by Dr. Theophilus Mack at St. Catharine's General and

Marine Hospital. Many other schools would be established across the country in the years that followed, and this would ensure that hospitals would secure the kind of nursing support necessary to minister to the needs of the population in all areas of the country.

■ Nursing is Established in the West

Canadian nursing orders also established nursing services in the western part of the country as it opened up to settlement. In 1844, four Grey Nuns made the 2 month journey to St. Boniface, Manitoba in long canoes. After their arrival, they were immersed in caring for those desperately ill in a succession of epidemics. In the next 10 years, they would make 6000 visits to the sick in their homes (Gibbon and Mathewson, 1947). The Grey Nuns also were the pioneering nursing order that established health services in Alberta and Saskatchewan. Venturing to the Alberta region of the Northwest Territories in 1859 at the invitation of the bishop in the area, they arrived 5 years before the first resident physicians, when there was only a small Hudson's Bay trading post at Fort Edmonton. They established their first mission at Lac Ste.-Anne, moving four years later to St.-Albert. From there, they extended their services to the far north and to Saskatchewan. After the decision to route the Great Northern Railroad through Edmonton, the population of Edmonton increased exponentially, and the Grey Nuns were asked by the physicians who were practising in Edmonton to establish a hospital. Thus they moved the base of their operations once again, this time from St.-Albert to Edmonton to construct and operate the Edmonton General Hospital in 1895. The Grey Nuns would extend their mission of education and nursing services to a settlement in northern Saskatchewan 400 miles north of Saskatoon and to Fort Providence on Great Slave Lake. These pioneering orders of nuns required tremendous courage to venture to the largely uninhabited western regions of the country when they did, for the lives they took up were the harsh lives of pioneers, and their mission of healing made their existence even more challenging.

■ The Development of National and Provincial Professional Organizations

The impetus for the establishment of nursing organizations came largely from an important leader in British nursing and editor of the *British Journal of Nursing*, Mrs. Ethel Gordon Bedford Fenwick. Mrs. Bedford Fenwick thought that nurses should band together to discuss issues and pursue common goals at an international level. She attended the Congress of Charities, Corrections and Philanthropy in Chicago in 1893, and there she met with the major leaders in American nursing of the time, Isabel Hampton, Adelaide Nutting, and Lavinia Dock. (Two of these three leaders in nursing in the United States were Canadians, namely Isabel

Hampton and Adelaide Nutting.) These women had gone to the United States to enrol in nursing education programs and had stayed to take up important positions in the rapidly expanding profession. The goal of registration for nurses to raise the standard of professional nursing was a central issue, and these nursing leaders decided to work for the establishment of nursing organizations to mobilize support for the major goals of nurses.

The three American leaders took steps to form organizations to bring nurses together to discuss issues, to promote unity among nurses, and to develop a means of ensuring that the profession had an official voice on issues of concern in health and in nursing. The American Society of Superintendents of Training Schools for Nurses of the United States and Canada was formed in 1894, and Isabel Hampton became its first president (CNA, 1968). Alumnae associations also were seen as important nursing organizations, and the Nurses' Associated Alumnae of the United States and Canada was formed in 1896, again under the leadership of president Isabel Hampton Robb. This organization required members to have graduated from schools associated with hospitals with more than 100 beds and from a program that was 2 or more years duration. At first this organization sought to improve standards of education, but as this was difficult for a voluntary organization, and as these members were graduate nurses, they turned their attention to supporting registration for nurses.

The 1893 meeting of the four nursing leaders also led to the formation of an international organization, the International Council of Nurses (ICN) in 1899, with Britain, the United States, and Germany as charter members. Although Canada was not a charter member because it had not yet established a national nursing organization, Mary Agnes Snively, Director of Nursing of the Toronto General Hospital, became the first honourary treasurer of the ICN in 1899. Miss Snively would be influential in organizing the Canadian Association of Superintendents of Training Schools for Nurses, the first national nursing organization in Canada in 1907, and she would serve as its first president. The next year, the organization invited representatives from nursing groups across the country to meet to establish a national association of nurses. The Provisional Society of the Canadian National Association of Trained Nurses (CNATN) thus was founded with Mary Agnes Snively as founding president. The CNATN applied for membership in the ICN the next year and was formally welcomed to membership in 1909 at the ICN meeting in London (CNA, 1968). A full-time executive secretary of the organization, Jean Wilson, was appointed in 1923 when the national office opened in Winnipeg. The office later moved to Montreal and then to Ottawa. However, publication of the *Canadian Nurse* had begun much earlier, in 1905. This is understandable because the need for communication between Canadian nurses was great, and travel was difficult and expensive. Membership in the CNATN of affiliated organizations grew from 28 in 1911 to 52 in 1924, when the organization became the Canadian Nurses Association. In 1930 the CNA became a federation of the provincial nurses' associations, and as a result of this reorganization, nurses became members of the national organization by virtue of membership in their provincial professional association. More recently, the two territorial nursing organizations were welcomed to membership in the CNA federation.

The first meeting of the Provisional Council of the University Schools and Departments of Nursing was held on June 20, 1942, when representatives of 11 university schools and departments of nursing met to consider issues of common concern in university nursing education. Representatives of eight of these academic units had met 1 year earlier, a meeting that had been called by the executive of the CNA to consider federal proposals for financial assistance for university schools of nursing prompted by the severe shortage of nurses in the postwar period (Kirkwood and Bouchard, 1992, pp. 5-7). At the outset and for some years thereafter, group members differed about whether the group should meet independently of the CNA and whether the group could appropriately act as the official voice of university nursing education when group members were struggling to establish the legitimacy of their discipline and their academic units within their universities.

■ The Struggle for Registration

The struggle for registration of nurses was the unifying theme of the development of the early nursing organizations and is an inherent part of the evolution of nursing as a profession. Nurses believed strongly that to serve the public appropriately, they needed to gain control over the practice of their profession to ensure that recognized standards of practice were upheld and that untrained, incompetent, or unethical practitioners were not allowed to practise as nurses. Although the international and national organizations were organized as a part of the attempt to secure registration for nurses, nurses soon recognized that the case for the legitimacy of legislation for the registration of nurses would have to be made at the provincial level because jurisdiction over health was in the hands of the provinces. The first act governing nursing registration was passed in Nova Scotia in 1910, and all provinces had such acts by 1922, when Ontario passed its registration law. All of the initial pieces of legislation covered permissive registration, or protection of title only. The crusade for registration coincided with efforts to enfranchise women across the country. Women in Canada gained the right to vote in federal elections on May 24, 1918, and all of the provinces passed legislation between 1916 and 1940 permitting women to vote in provincial elections (Bashevkin, 1991, p. 420). In addition, the Person's Case came before the Supreme Court of Canada on April 24, 1928, when five Alberta women challenged the 1876 British Common Law ruling that "Women are persons in matters of pains and penalties, but are not persons in matters of rights and privileges." The question they asked was "Does the word 'person' in Section 24 of The British North America Act include female persons?"(Government of Alberta, 1991, pp. 2-3). Although the Supreme Court ruled that it did not, the decision was overturned by the Privy Council of Britain on October 18, 1929. This opened the way for women to be appointed and elected to public office in Canada.

The quest for mandatory registration, or protection of the practice of nursing, would come later, after nursing had undergone considerable development and evolution as a professional discipline. Legislation incorporating mandatory registration requires a definition of nursing and a description of the scope of nursing practice in the legislation. The first mandatory nursing act was passed in 1953 in Newfoundland, and the next would not be passed until almost 20 years later in Prince Edward Island in 1972. The legislation passed in Quebec in 1973, with significant amendments in 1974, was comprehensive, was the first to incorporate a detailed definition of nursing, and mandated an inspection role for the professional association in monitoring standards of practice. Although the Manitoba statute passed in 1980 is permissive, it does require employers to demonstrate that those employed as registered nurses are, in fact, registered. Alberta passed a mandatory statute, the Nursing Profession Act, in 1983, and similar acts were passed in New Brunswick in 1984, Nova Scotia in 1985, and Saskatchewan and British Columbia in 1988. Thus the only two provinces that have not yet developed mandatory legislation for the regulation of those practising nursing are Manitoba and Ontario. The movement for mandatory registration for nurses also coincided with the reawakening of the women's movement in North America from the late 1960s onward, characterized by a drive for greater rights and opportunities for women in all areas of human activity. Bashevkin has commented on the conditions or forces that facilitate the struggle for equality by women: "Feminism, like other reform movements, has emerged during periods in which society tolerates searching self-criticism in the belief that purposeful change can bring about indisputable improvement" (1991, p. 413).

■ Nursing During Military Conflicts

Nurses have played primary roles during military conflicts in which Canadian forces have seen active service. The earliest involvement of nurses could be considered the roles played by the nursing sisters of the Hôtel Dieu hospitals of Montreal and Quebec during the conflict between the English and the French between 1756 and 1763. The Northwest Rebellion of 1885 was the first military involvement after Confederation in which two groups of nurses provided service (CNA, 1968). In 1898, the Victorian Order of Nurses sent nurses attached to the Yukon Military Force and were lauded for their efforts (Gibbon and Mathewson, 1947). In the next year, a group of Canadian nurses was sent by the Canadian Government to aid in the British effort in the Boer War, and the first group of four nurses was sent to assist in South Africa under the leadership of Georgina Fane Pope, a nurse from Prince Edward Island who had been educated at Bellevue Hospital (Gibbon and Mathewson, 1947). The efforts of these nurses were viewed as so essential to operations during the war that the Canadian Army Medical Corps decided that an army nursing service should be a part of the permanent corps. Consequently, Georgina Pope and Margaret Macdonald were appointed to the permanent staff in 1906 (Gibbon and Mathewson, 1947).

When World War I broke out, the Canadian Army Nursing Corps consisted of five nurses, but within 3 weeks of the declaration of war, thousands of nurses had volunteered for military service overseas. Margaret Macdonald was appointed Matron-in-Chief of the Army Nursing Corps at the outset, and some 1800 nurses saw service during the war, including 14 nurses who lost their lives in the sinking of the Canadian hospital ship Llandovery Castle (CNA, 1968). After World War I, when Canadian nurses had distinguished themselves by their dedication and the quality of care they gave, a permanent nursing corps was maintained by the Royal Canadian Army Medical Corps, and a registry was maintained of nurses who could be available for active service if war broke out. By the time World War II broke out, Canadian nurses were seen as a critical component of the hospital services established to provide care for those wounded on the battlefield. Up to this time, nurses in military service had held the relative rank of officers but were not accorded the rank and privileges that accompanied officer status. About halfway through the war, the Privy Council ordered this changed, and nurses then were granted commissions equal to those of other commissioned officers. Nurses in Britain and the United States did not secure this status until the conclusion of the war (CNA, 1968). Permanent positions for military nurses have continued to constitute part of the armed forces that Canada has maintained during peacetime.

■ The Emergence of Public Health Nursing

Public health nursing emerged as an important and specialized area of nursing in the early decades of the twentieth century. The concept of preventing illness and the spread of disease from one individual to another by educating people about appropriate health behaviour was not well recognized until after scientists made several important advances. These included acceptance of the germ theory and modes of transmission of infectious diseases through human contact, droplet spread, and still other modes of dissemination of causative agents. Some of the earliest public health nursing involved visiting tuberculosis patients in their homes and teaching them how to care for themselves to promote their health and prevent further problems. The first school nurses were appointed in Hamilton in 1909 and

Toronto in 1910. Lina Rogers, a graduate of the Hospital for Sick Children, achieved international recognition because she was able to demonstrate that there was a relationship between the absence of children from school and lack of medical care. Her work with the School Nursing Service of the Toronto Board of Education led to the recruitment of nurses and dentists whose mandate was education of children and their families about proper hygiene to prevent disease. The Nursing Service was later transferred to the Health Department and served as a model for the rest of the country as the movement to improve the public health gained momentum (Gibbon and Mathewson, 1947).

As a consequence of the great loss of life of enlisted men during World War I and coincidental to growing understanding of the concept of prevention, society increasingly recognized the importance of health and prevention of illness. The health of mothers and children was seen as vital to the nation, and the importance of ensuring their health through prevention of disease was increasingly valued. Consequently, the Canadian Red Cross Society provided funds to initiate courses in public health nursing in five universities across the country at the Universities of British Columbia, Alberta, and Toronto, and at McGill and Dalhousie Universities. In addition, the Red Cross Society of London, Ontario provided funds to allow the University of Western Ontario to develop a certificate course in public health nursing (Canadian Red Cross Society, 1962). Gradually these certificate programs grew into baccalaureate degree programs in nursing, and public health continued to form an essential component of the baccalaureate nursing curriculum as the programs developed further. The Victorian Order of Nurses also supported public health nursing education by providing bursaries for study of public health beginning in 1921 (Gibbon, 1947).

However, despite the fact that society recognized the importance of public health, legislation intended to develop hospital and acute care services after the second World War somewhat reduced the role of health promotion and disease prevention efforts based in the community over the next half century. This has occurred even though the federal government has attempted to focus attention on the importance of healthy lifestyles and the understanding of health behaviour to promote health and prevent disease beginning some 2 decades ago (Lalonde, 1975; Epp, 1986). Skyrocketing costs of health services provided through the acute-care model have increased recognition of the value of community-based care, where emphasis has been placed on health education, health promotion, and prevention of disease. The adoption of a primary health care approach in which nurses have essential roles means radical alterations in the existing system. However, a community-based approach holds the potential for gains in health and decreases in health spending through more efficient utilization of health professionals and by encouraging more client involvement and control in decisions concerning their own health.

■ The Struggle for Recognition and Equality

The struggle by nurses for recognition as health professionals has stretched over the last century. The concurrent drive for equality of women undoubtedly was an important contributing factor in the campaign by nurses for registration. When nursing first became recognized as a legitimate profession for women, it was only the second field of endeavour to open to women. The drive for registration of nurses occurred concurrently with the effort to gain the vote for women by the suffragists. However, women were far from achieving anything approaching true equality and were prevented by both convention and regulation from working after marriage. Their entry into the workplace in large numbers was produced first by the needs of the country during the second world war to fulfil roles in business and government formerly performed by men who were now away at war. However, after the war, women were told to go home and care for home and family, and disincentives were put in place to encourage them to vacate their positions in favour of the returning soldiers.

The discovery of oral contraceptives and their widespread availability to women brought a new era of emancipation for women through a childbearing timetable they could control. Nursing also developed in the expansive years of the 1960s and 1970s, retaining its acceptability as a profession for women. When nontraditional occupations began to open to women, the new women's movement began to look less favourably on traditional occupations for women such as nursing and teaching, and began to cast them in stereotypical roles that did not reflect the changing nature of their professional disciplines. The relationship between the women's movement and nursing has been termed "the uneasy alliance" by Vance, Talbott, McBride, and Mason (1985). However, the fact that the new feminists did not understand the profession and its work was probably a reflection of the image of nursing in the larger community. Recognizing this, the profession has attempted to develop public understanding of the traditional and changing roles of nurses in the health-care system.

Development of Nursing Unions

Strong organizations have developed to engage in collective bargaining for nurses in recent decades through strikes by large groups of nurses to increase remuneration and improve working conditions. Many instances can be documented of nurses' confrontations with their employers over wages and conditions the nurses believed to be unfair. These have included both threats to strike and actual withdrawals of services and have involved both graduate nurses and students, the latter constituting the nursing workforce in hospitals before the 1940s. One threatened strike that was averted involved the 10 nurses on the nursing staff of the General Hospital in St. John's in 1919, who sent a letter to the Board of

Governors of the hospital requesting an increase in salary: "When the nurses had not received any reply by 20 June, they informed the Board of Governors that if a pay increase was not received by the following Sunday they would withdraw their services" (White, 1994, p. 91). Many other examples of conflict with employers can be documented in the early history of the profession. In the past 3 decades, Hibberd has referred to 32 strikes by nurses in Canada between 1966 and 1982 and another 5 between 1985 and 1989, of which 4 were major provincial work stoppages (1992).

The CNA approved the principle of collective bargaining for nurses in the 1940s and affirmed that the bargaining agent in each province should be the professional nurses association. The association also went on record as supporting a no-strike policy, an action that later would become controversial and would be repealed in the 1960s. The passage of the federal Labour Relations Act in 1944 gave federal employees, including nurses who were federal employees, collective bargaining rights and likely influenced the CNA's action to support collective bargaining for nurses in the same year. The first nursing organization to apply successfully for certification as a bargaining unit was the Registered Nurses Association of British Columbia in 1946. Eventually nurses in all provinces gained the right to bargain collectively and were able to have their organizations certified as bargaining agents. In 1973, the Supreme Court of Canada ruled on a lawsuit brought against the Saskatchewan Registered Nurses Association (SRNA) by the Service Employees International Union (SEIU) over the appropriateness of the SRNA to be the bargaining agent for nurses because the SRNA board included management nurses among its number. These nurses were deemed by the SEIU to be in a conflict of interest in considering questions relative to collective bargaining because they would be upholding the interests of employers at the same time they were asked to consider the interest of the nurses. The Supreme Court decision supported the SEIU's case, and as a result the separation of nursing unions from professional associations was ensured from that point onward.

Nurses have developed strong unions that have become highly visible across the country in arguing for the rights of nurses for fair and equitable salaries and working conditions. The groundwork for these new organizations was laid in the provincial professional associations, and they would move in new directions as they developed their own identities as independent organizations. They have, in fact, earned the respect of many other groups in the union movement through their clear and straightforward focus on the interests of their members. As they have gained experience in all aspects of the labour relations movement, nursing unions have attempted to strike a balance between the need to demand appropriate remuneration and working conditions for their members and the professional needs of members who care about their clients and their clients' needs.

■ The Past and the Future

All nurses can be proud of the history of nursing in Canada. Nurses have provided nursing care of the highest quality to people since the time of the earliest settlements in New France. The nature of the service has developed over time as nurses acquired more knowledge and adapted their care to the needs of the people they served. From the earliest times, the major goal of nurses' work was to care for those who suffered from infectious diseases, as these diseases were the primary causes of morbidity and mortality before the advent of antibiotics. As a part of the work they performed in communities and in hospitals with infectious diseases, nurses also have performed activities to promote health and prevent disease. Nurses have volunteered their services in large numbers during times of major conflicts in which the country was at war, and their service has been widely lauded as distinguished. Nurses also have been critical to the implementation of new and lifesaving technology in tertiary care centres in the past 3 decades. Altruism has characterized nurses and nursing over time, and although the health-care system is undergoing rapid change brought by the health-care reform that is sweeping the country, nurses undoubtedly will continue to play significant roles in the system that emerges.

■ REFERENCES

Bashevkin, S.B. (1991). Independence versus partisanship: Dilemmas in the political history of women in English Canada. In V. Strong-Boag & A.C. Fellman (Eds.), *Rethinking Canada: The promise of women's history* (pp. 413-445). Toronto: Copp Clark Pitman.

Canadian Nurses Association. (1968). *The leaf and the lamp*. Ottawa: The Association.

Canadian Red Cross Society. (1962). *The role of one voluntary organization in Canada's health services: A brief presented to the Royal Commission on Health Services.* Toronto: The Society.

Epp, J. (1986). *Achieving health for all: A framework for health promotion.* Ottawa: Health and Welfare Canada.

Gibbon, J.M. (1947). *The Victorian Order of Nurses: 50th Anniversary, 1897-1947.* Montreal: Southam Press.

Gibbon, J.M. & Mathewson, M.S. (1947). *Three centuries of Canadian nursing.* Toronto: The Macmillan Co.

Government of Alberta. (1991). *The Persons case.* Edmonton: Government of Alberta.

Hibberd, J.M. (1992). Strikes by nurses. In A.J. Baumgart & J. Larsen (Eds.), *Canadian nursing faces the future* (pp. 575-596). Toronto: Mosby–Year Book.

Kirkwood, R. & Bouchard, J. (1992). *"Take counsel with one another": A beginning history of the Canadian Association of University Schools of Nursing, 1942-1992.* Ottawa: Canadian Association of University Schools of Nursing.

Lalonde, M. (1975). *A New Perspective on the Health of Canadians.* Ottawa: Health and Welfare Canada.

Millman, M.B. (1965). In G. Griffin & J. Griffin (Eds.), *Jensen's history and trends of professional nursing* (pp. 423-439). St. Louis: Mosby–Year Book.

Parkman, F. (1897). *The Jesuits in North America in the seventeenth century.* Boston: Little Brown & Co.

Vance, C., Talbott, S., McBride, A., & Mason, D. (1985). An uneasy alliance: Nursing and the women's movement. *Nursing Outlook, 33*(6), 281-285.

White, L. (1994). Who's in charge here? The General Hospital School of Nursing, St. John's, Newfoundland, 1903-1930. *Canadian Bulletin of Medical History, 11*(1), 91-118.

ETHICAL AND LEGAL QUESTIONS IN NURSING PRACTICE

2

JANNETTA MACPHAIL AND JANET ROSS KERR

All citizens are responsible for their own actions under the law, and professionals have additional obligations to their clients by virtue of their specialized knowledge and skills. A professional whose performance of duties is believed by a client to be remiss may be called to account for actions in a court of law. In certain situations where an individual's actions are considered negligent, a suit may be brought by one person against another, or, in the case of a criminal matter, charges may be laid by the police. Our society commonly believes that people have certain ethical and moral obligations to one another. While some of these are accepted as general principles of behaviour, obligations of an ethical or moral nature generally are less defined than those of a legal nature, as legal obligations between people under the law often are spelled out in written form.

Ethical responsibilities are not as clearly defined, and ethical dilemmas in health care are common in our era of lifesaving technology in which public awareness of ethical obligations between people is increasing. Indeed, people all over the world increasingly are realizing that people and nations, regardless of race, culture, or financial status, cannot exist in isolation. Each person depends on others for survival ecologically. As pollution and other life-threatening problems on the planet become more critical, conflicts between nations will be mediated by the morality of relationships between people all over the world. In the perspective of the world as a global village, the economic environment may take a back seat to such developments.

Although legal and ethical issues in nursing are similar in Canada and the United States, the legal systems and the application of ethical principles to nursing practice are unique in each country. Although the legal systems of both countries are based on English common law, differences in regulations and procedures governing the justice system, the courts, and professionals are considerable. In addition, although the traditions and trends of the law bear some similarity to one another, the cases from which precedents arise are clearly different in each country. Because ethics as a discipline is much less clear-cut and involves difficult situations and dilemmas where it is difficult to reach readily acceptable solutions, in some ways developments in the United States and Canada have many common elements, and developments have influence across borders. However, in the discussion of major ethical and legal issues in this chapter, the unique influence of the Canadian context will form the basis of the discussion.

Although health professionals always have encountered ethical issues and dilemmas in practice and have had to address difficult ethical questions, the issues and dilemmas today are more complex than ever. Factors contributing to this complexity are the rapidly expanding body of health care knowledge and the development of technologies to save, generate, or prolong life. At the same time, changes in societal values have increased the recognition of individual rights and freedoms and have heightened awareness of both the importance of and the need to protect those rights. Better-informed consumers who are more questioning and who expect to be more involved in decisions about their own lives and health have changed both the context and resolution of ethical dilemmas. As a result of the eradication of many infectious and other diseases, improved control over still other diseases, and improved living standards, the human life span has been lengthened considerably during this century. Because people are living longer, new ethical questions about the prolongation of life have been raised. Because health care costs consume an increasing proportion of the Gross Domestic Product and because of the high cost of new technologies, society has realized that choices must be made in a climate of limited and finite resources. These questions about priorities in the health-care system and about the best allocation of resources require difficult decisions about who will receive care and under what conditions.

Health professionals face many dilemmas in everyday practice. Who decides what is right for the individual or family involved? Is there always a right answer? Curtin defines ethics as "a discipline in which we attempt to identify, organize, analyze, and justify human acts by applying certain principles to determine the right thing to do in a given situation" (1985, p. 1). Thus the discipline of ethics is concerned with judgment of actions, not judgment of human beings. However, even when the best principles and the best intentions are applied to certain situations, the outcomes will not necessarily satisfy any or all of the parties involved. Because people are all different, approaches and responses in similar but difficult ethical dilemmas are bound to be diverse.

■ Basic Ethical Theories and Principles

A prerequisite to applying ethics in nursing is having a theoretical base in ethics, just as basic knowledge in the biological and behavioural sciences is requisite to the application of principles and concepts from those sciences to nursing. Without a theoretical base, discussion of ethical issues may be merely sharing of opinions. Two basic theoretical approaches are: (1) teleological, which is goal-directed or consequence-oriented, and (2) deontological, which is duty-oriented or focused on rules. Kluge (1992) identifies the difference between the two approaches "in the sorts of considerations they find relevant in reaching their conclusions" (p. 17). The teleological approach focuses on the anticipated outcome of actions, whereas "the deontological approach concentrates on balancing rights and duties . . . and considers them independently of outcome considerations" (Kluge, 1992, p. 17).

Although providing a theoretical base for ethical decision making in this text is not feasible, basic concepts of ethics can be identified. They include: (1) *personhood*, of which self-awareness is a basic quality (Storch, 1982); (2) *autonomy*, which implies not only freedom to decide and to act, but also to acknowledge and respect the dignity and autonomy of others (Francoeur, 1983); however, a health professional "has the obligation to intervene if the patient's choice is not in his/her best interests, particularly when there is reason to believe that the benefit is very great and harm would be significant" (Fry as interpreted by Reid, 1992, p. 26); (3) *veracity*, which includes obligation to tell the truth and to use good judgment in determining what the patient wants to know or can withstand; (4) *paternalism*, which refers to restricting the rights of an individual without his/her consent with the justification of trying to do good, such as not telling a person about his/her diagnosis and condition because of a poor prognosis; (5) *confidentiality*, which must be maintained but balanced against the rights of others, including society (Francoeur, 1983); (6) *beneficence*, or doing what is best for an individual while balancing the risks and benefits in a given situation; (7) *nonmaleficence*, or not inflicting intentional harm or risk of harm and preventing evil or harm whenever possible; and (8) *justice*, which means ensuring that individuals get what they deserve according to individual need, worth, and merit and enforcing the concept of distributive justice, which "has to do with the distribution of good and evil, of burdens and benefits in any society when resources are limited" (Davis and Aroskar, 1983, p. 45). The question of justice is an ethical dilemma frequently encountered today with cutbacks in funding and layoff of nurses, which may require nurses to make difficult decisions about apportioning care when all needs cannot be met.

Nurses must have knowledge of basic ethical concepts to be able to address the increasingly complex issues they encounter daily in practice settings. Although one tends to consider only the ethical dilemmas faced in acute care settings, the issues are different but equally complex for practitioners in long-term care settings and in the community, because of increased longevity, early discharge from hospital, and the use of technologies in the home that previously were limited to acute-care settings. Robillard et al. (1989) point out that little research has focused on the ethical issues in primary care, although most health care is provided in primary care settings. Their study revealed that the issues are most frequently pragmatic, not dramatic, and are concerned with "patient self-determination, adequacy of care and professional responsibility, and distribution of resources" (Robillard et al., 1989, p. 9). Thus nurses practising in all types of health-care settings need a knowledge base in ethical concepts and principles, as well as support and expert resources to assist them in ensuring that basic human rights are recognized and respected.

■ An Overview of the Canadian Legal System

The origins of the Canadian legal system can be found in English common law and Roman law. Quebec provincial law is derived from Roman law, the basis of the latter being found in The Twelve Tables of Rome (450 BC), Justinian's Code (533 AD), and the Napoleonic Code of 1804 (Merryman, 1969). The roots of English common law began more recently with the Norman conquest of 1066 (Plucknett, 1956). The law sets the parameters for human activity by defining rules for judging the acceptability of individual and corporate behaviour. In a sense, the law defines our culture by outlining how we may behave based on certain social values and by providing deterrents to deviance from acceptable behaviour. The institutions of the law in our society are the provincial legislatures and the Parliament of Canada, which are entrusted with the creation of law through the passage of acts; the police forces across the country, whose mandate is the enforcement of the law; the courts as the arbitrators of disputes; and the prisons, which are responsible for applying punishments for breaking the law.

The major types of law are case law and enacted law. The traditions of English common law are such that case law is dominant, while in the Roman civil law tradition, enacted law is the primary form of law, which is mainly statutory. In Canada, these two traditions survive with the two founding nations. The Quebec civil code is based on the Roman tradition, while in the rest of Canada, the traditions of English common law prevail. According to Dais (1973), enacted law has become more important in areas where the traditions of common law are the primary form of the law. However, these usually do not extend to codes such as those customary under Roman traditions, which incorporate detailed descriptions of daily life.

Although the courts often are considered the major component of the judicial system, other important components include the legal profession and the adversary system. The major types of law include civil or private law, which incorporates contract, tort, and property law; and public law, which includes constitutional, administrative, and criminal law. International law involves both of these types of law. Where the law is concerned with individuals, it is considered private law, and where it is concerned with governments, it falls within public law (Dais, 1973). In Canada, jury trials are reserved primarily for criminal cases and are used for very few civil cases. This is different from the United States, where the traditions of English common law also prevail, and where jury trials are used more often in civil cases. Because of the considerable expenses associated with jury trials, the Canadian approach tends to be less costly.

■ Legal Responsibilities of Nurses

Nurses have important legal obligations to the public as professionals who have close relationships with people. As health care has changed, so have nurses' responsibilities toward their clients. In tertiary care settings, nurses have become responsible for procedures that are highly technical and that carry considerably greater risk than was true in the past. Even in community settings, this holds true in many situations. Thus nurses daily have more chance of violating the rights of others, simply because of the nature of the acts for which they have become responsible. Just as for physicians and other health professionals, the public expects that nurses will practise safely and competently according to the ethical principles that have been identified previously. When cases are in dispute, courts look to the concept of a reasonable standard of care in deciding whether a particular nurse acted prudently in a particular situation.

■ Clients' Rights and Nurses' Obligations in Health Care

Basic Human Rights in Health Care

Basic human rights in health care, which increasingly are recognized today, are the right to be informed, the right to be respected, and the right to self-determination. Each has great implications in ethical decision-making and in the responsibility of health professionals to protect rights. These rights also cause debate over ethical issues and are the bases for confrontation between nurses and physicians. For example, nurses and physicians may differ about the meaning of being informed and whose responsibility it is to inform the individual and family. A confrontation may result from the witholding of information by a physician who believes it is in the best interest of the patient, when the nurse believes that the patient should be informed and is asked directly for such information. The right to be informed has increased the need to obtain informed consent before medical interventions are instituted and before patients are asked to participate in research. Until the 1970s, there was no expectation or requirement to obtain informed consent for participation in research, and people sometimes were exploited. For example, in an experiment at the Allen Memorial Institute in Montreal in the late 1940s, patients were administered mind-altering drugs, such as lysergic acid diethylamide (LSD), which had far-reaching effects. Patients sought and obtained recompense through legal action in the 1980s.

The right to be respected has great implications in approaches to patients and is related to the right to be informed. Providing an interpretation of care and explaining medical conditions in understandable language are two methods of showing respect for an individual. Respect also has implications for confidentiality, which has been a problem in the sharing of information among health professionals. Although nurses and physicians may respect confidentiality to the point of not sharing information with people outside the health professions, they tend to share information openly in discussions where it can be overheard. Confidentiality also requires that written records be carefully protected, which has great implications in the expanding use of computers for storage and retrieval of patient data.

The right to self-determination implies that individuals or families have the right to make decisions about matters that affect their health and their lives. Ensuring that this right is protected is complex; for example, it involves deciding whether an individual is capable of making decisions and, if not, who should be involved in the decision-making. Making decisions about matters that affect a patient's health and life includes giving people the opportunity to decide not to have treatment recommended by a physician. This is a difficult situation for health professionals because they face an individual refusing treatment that they believe is best for that individual. In some circumstances, refusing the treatment is logical because of the individual's prognosis and desire not to undergo adverse side effects known to result from the treatment, such as cancer therapy in cases where the disease has progressed beyond redemption. On the other hand, some individuals choose to be treated almost to the end, even if there is no hope of cure or remission.

Self-determination is not limited to life-and-death matters; it also involves decisions about life-styles. For example, individuals make decisions to continue lifestyles and behaviour patterns that are known to be detrimental to their health and well-being, such as smoking, overeating, excessive drinking, refusing to wear seat belts, and engaging in sexual relations with people likely to be carriers of the acquired immunodeficiency virus. Although efforts to educate the public about the hazards of such habits are succeeding, many people still choose to do things that are harmful to their health.

Codes of Ethics

A code of ethics is one of the characteristics of a profession. It is defined by the profession through the professional association and is designed to inform members of the profession and society about the profession's expectations in ethical matters. For many years, physicians have taken the Hippocratic Oath on graduating from medical school. Although it provides some ethical direction, it also can be interpreted as committing the physician to save or prolong life at any cost. This is one of the factors leading to stressful interprofessional relationships when physicians consider decisions about prolonging life to be their responsibility, and nurses believe the individual and/or family should be involved in making decisions that affect their lives.

In 1955 the Canadian Nurses Association (CNA) adopted the code of ethics developed in 1953 by the International Council of Nurses (ICN) and replaced in 1973 by the *ICN Code for Nurses—Ethical Concepts Applied to Nursing*, to guide Canadian nurses in ethical decision-making. In 1978 the CNA membership decided to make the development of a national code of ethics a priority; the first *CNA Code of Ethics for Nursing* was approved in 1980. It was revised in 1985 and again in 1991 based on input from nurses using it in practice and was distributed to all CNA members with *The Canadian Nurse*, CNA's official journal received monthly by members.

> This Code expresses and seeks to clarify the obligation of nurses to use their knowledge and skills for the benefit of others, to minimize harm, to respect client autonomy and to provide fair and just care for their clients. For those entering the profession, this Code identifies the basic moral commitments of nursing and may serve as a source of education and reflection. For those within the profession, the Code also serves as a basis for self-evaluation and for peer review. For those outside the profession, this Code may serve to establish expectations for the ethical conduct of nurses (CNA, November 1991, p. ii).

The Code presents values, or broad ideals, and obligations arising from each value that provide direction in particular circumstances. Some values pertain to clients or patients; other values are concerned with nursing roles and relationships. An example of a value and the obligations deriving therefrom is shown in the box on page 23.

Although codes of ethics may or may not be part of statutory regulations, most provinces have a statutory requirement within the act governing the nursing profession that mandates that nurses uphold ethical standards as defined by the nursing profession. This means that not only are individual nurses expected to uphold the precepts contained in codes of ethics, but also colleagues are held accountable for adhering to them. Thus codes of ethics contain statements of moral accountability that "provide an enforceable standard of minimally decent conduct that allows the profession to discipline those who clearly fall below the standard . . . (and indicate) some of the ethical considerations professionals must take into account in deciding on conduct" (Benjamin and Curtis, 1986, p. 6).

◼ **A VALUE AND RESULTING OBLIGATIONS FOR NURSES**

Value IV...Dignity of Clients

The nurse is guided by consideration for the dignity of clients.

Obligations

1. Nursing care must be done with consideration for the personal modesty of clients.
2. A nurse's conduct at all times should acknowledge the client as a person. For example, discussion of care in the presence of the client should actively involve that client.
3. Nurses have a responsibility to intervene when other participants in the health care system fail to respect any aspect of client dignity.
4. As ways of dealing with death and the dying person change, nursing is challenged to find new ways to preserve human values, autonomy, and dignity. In assisting the dying client, measures must be taken to afford the clients as much comfort, dignity, and freedom from anxiety and pain as possible. Special consideration must be given to the need of the client's family or significant others to cope with their loss.

*Canadian Nurses Association. (1991). *Code of ethics for nursing*. Ottawa: the Association, p.7.

Because of the complexity of the ethical dilemmas nurses confront today, they need more than a code of ethics. Storch (1982) believes that at least four conditions are necessary for ethical decision-making: (1) desire and commitment to do what is right and good; (2) knowledge of relevant facts of the particular situation; (3) clarity of thought, rather than emotionalism, in dealing with the facts; and (4) some understanding of basic principles or concepts of ethics. In recent years, nurses and other health professionals have recognized the importance of examining and clarifying values that may influence their actions and of becoming more sensitive to the values of their patients. Rather than prescribing a set of values, values-clarification strategies increasingly are being used in both nursing education programs and continuing education programs for practising nurses.

The Right to Make Choices in Relation to Death

Death and dying give rise to many ethical issues and dilemmas. Davis and Aroskar (1983) identify three issues: (1) possible interventions by health professionals, such as resuscitation and passive euthanasia; (2) possible interventions by the family or significant others, such as helping a terminally ill person to hasten death and end suffering; and (3) possible interventions by the afflicted person, such as suicide, use of a living will, and claiming a right to die.

The word *euthanasia* is derived from Greek, meaning good or pleasant death. Is death ever preferable to life? That question is difficult to answer. One must consider each situation and distinguish it from the interests and values of the care provider and the institution. Some think that euthanasia should be considered only for those who can ask to die, which would eliminate newborns, infants, and individuals kept alive by machines and unable to speak for themselves. Others believe that in certain circumstances some severely deformed newborns should be allowed to die by withdrawing or withholding treatments, and that the decision should be made by the parents and their professional advisors, who are usually physicians (Duff and Campbell, 1973; McCormick, 1974; Shaw, 1973).

Passive euthanasia, or "letting someone die," may be carried out by not initiating treatment, with or without consent of the individual. These measures, although used in some hospitals, are still morally controversial. Active euthanasia is providing an individual with the means to end life or directly bringing about the individual's death with or without consent (Brody, 1976). How does the concept of protecting human rights fit into euthanasia? Does a person ever have the right to die? Can one refuse life-saving treatment? Is the lack of clear-cut policies and guidelines to help health professionals address such complex questions a reflection of there being no right or wrong answer? Some believe that death should never be hastened; others believe that a person whose death is imminent should be allowed to die to relieve pain and suffering, and that the right to refuse treatment should be respected. Some fear that if euthanasia as a kindly act—beneficent euthanasia—can be morally justified, euthanasia for other purposes also may be justified and practised (Dyck, 1975).

■ Nurses' Actions Under the Law

Consent to Nursing Care

The right to be free from interference is a fundamental human right. Because nursing in some settings may involve a great deal of touching of others, one must recognize that the nurse must obtain consent from the client before touching occurs. Battery is a tort that involves intentional touching of another person, and there is no requirement that the person be injured as a result of the touching. In practice, clients rarely bring legal proceedings if they have not suffered serious harm as a result of touching. However, every nurse must be very careful to explain nursing procedures to clients and to obtain consent before initiating a procedure. Effective communication between nurses and clients is vital, and explaining and obtaining the patient's permission to carry out procedures are essential parts of this communication.

Consent to care may be expressed, implied, or inferred. In the past, nurses often have relied on implied consent for procedures. However, Philpott (1985) has stated that in the absence of emergency conditions or in the case of procedures involving considerable risk, one is unwise to rely on implied consent. The six elements that must be present in legal consent are:

1. The consent must be genuine and voluntary.
2. The procedure must not be an illegal procedure.
3. The consent must authorize the particular performer of the treatment or care.
4. The consenter must have legal capacity to consent.
5. The consenter must have the necessary mental competency to consent.
6. The consenter must be informed (p. 57).

Even though such issues as age, health, and mental status of clients may make it difficult for the nurse to obtain informed consent, it is nonetheless essential to do so in the appropriate way for the circumstances present in each situation.

Confidentiality

Nurses often think of confidentiality as an exclusively ethical issue. However, the client's right to confidentiality is embedded in the provincial hospital acts. Acts regulating nursing also specify the nurse's professional responsibility to maintain client confidentiality. A nurse who fails to carry out this responsibility may be subject to allegations of professional misconduct. The provinces of Quebec, British Columbia, Manitoba, and Saskatchewan also protect the right of privacy by statutes. Provinces where the only references to privacy are in the hospital acts do not provide the same level of protection. Section 7 of *The Charter of Rights and Freedoms* contains a section that has not yet been explored and that may be used in future challenges made under the charter; this is found in the statement: "Everyone has the right to life, liberty and security of the person and the right not to be deprived thereof except in accordance with the principles of fundamental justice" (p. 11).

There are certain exceptions to the responsibility to maintain confidentiality. These include situations in which the client gives consent to disclose personal information to those not named in the provincial hospital act, statutory provisions for reporting certain diseases and child abuse to certain health and social agencies, and court orders for the purpose of obtaining health records for the use of plaintiffs or defendants in trials. Although the client's right to view personal health records has been a controversial issue in the past for those pursuing legal action against a health care agency or its employees, society increasingly is recognizing that clients have a right to see their records. As new legislation on confidentiality is developed, this right is likely to be recognized.

Collaboration with Physicians

Nurses work in close collaboration with physicians and, in cases where physicians have communicated their wishes for a patient's treatment to nurses over the telephone, misunderstandings occasionally have occurred. In any situation where written directions for treatment are not made at the time directions are given, the potential for misinterpretation exists. Where telephone orders are acceptable within a health care agency, a nurse may be liable if there is later disagreement with a physician over the orders. The increasing complexity of health care means that risks for nurses also are increasing. If telephone orders are allowable in the health care agency, the agency should have a system for contemporaneous external validation of the orders to enhance safety for the client and to ensure that the nurse is not subject to unwarranted risk. This could take the form of taping and transcription of telephone orders or of having the order validated by a second nurse at the time it is given.

Nursing Documentation

The Supreme Court of Canada declared that nurses' notes were admissible in court in 1970 (*Ares v Venner*, 1970). This attests to the importance of nurses' records of the care provided to and progress made by clients in their care and means that nurses' notes could serve to support cases for or against nurses, physicians, or hospitals. The importance of "the virtues of accuracy, legibility, brevity practised faithfully by the nurse" in enhancing the value of nursing documentation to the care of the client has been underscored by Ross (1973, p. 102). In the event of "unusual occurrence" or "incident reports," which most often are written by nurses, the importance of a "cool, dispassionate, and thoughtful" approach to making a "factual, concise and totally objective" record of the event is supported by the fact that incident records could be introduced as evidence to support or defend a damage claim (Ross, 1973, pp. 102-103).

Problems with nurses' notes frequently have been the subject of criticism in court records of proceedings, thus underscoring the importance of the principles of recording previously described. Failure to record events immediately after they have happened can be a serious matter because individuals are likely to forget details that might be very important in a particular situation if time elapses between the time the event happened and the time it was described in a written record. Recording of care by someone other than the nurse who provided the care also casts doubt on the validity of the record. Care provided, but not recorded, is difficult to verify. The fact that cases often come to trial long after the events in dispute occurred makes it difficult for principals to remember critical details in such situations. The importance of a clear, comprehensive, and detailed written record cannot be overestimated. This does not mean that nurses should spend their time recording everything they do for clients. Many believe that this both wastes the time of the highly skilled professional nurse and is unnecessary. Charting by exception, a method by which only unusual occurrences and reactions are recorded, is becoming more common in health care agencies. Good judgment and considerable discretion, however, must be used in determining what should and should not be recorded.

The advent of computers in hospitals and other health agencies where nurses are employed is raising new issues. Legibility of records is no longer a problem, but issues of the nature and quality of the recording persist. Program parameters can be set so that one cannot alter the time notation on the record and/or add to the text of a record written at an earlier time. Although signatures may not be possible, identifying codes for each user may help to record the identity of the writer. Confidentiality of computerized records also is a potential problem because more people may have access to the record than was the case before computerization. When systems for client records are developed, limiting access to only those with a need for access is an important issue. Storing records in a computerized file rather than in hard copy will minimize the space required to store large numbers of records and may improve access to a client's health history.

Negligence

Negligence, or that which a reasonable and prudent nurse would or would not do in particular health care circumstances, is the basis for most lawsuits against health professionals. Philpott has listed the conditions that must be present for a defendant to be held liable for damages in court:

1. The defendant must have a duty of care to the plaintiff.
2. The defendant's conduct must constitute a breach of that duty of care; that is, must have failed to comply with the required standard of care.
3. The plaintiff must have suffered an injury.
4. The negligent conduct must have been the proximate cause of the injury.
5. There must not have been contributory negligence on the part of the plaintiff and he must not have voluntarily assumed the risk (1985, p.25).

How the reasonable and prudent nurse would have acted in a similar situation is determined by courts in several ways. These include articles and books by nursing authors documenting the acceptability or lack of acceptability of certain practices, nursing practice standards developed by national and provincial professional nursing organizations, records of curriculum content in schools of nursing, and testimony by expert nurse witnesses. A nurse whose conduct is being scrutinized in court may expect that areas of interest to legal counsel will be the quality of practice, educational background, experience, and efforts to maintain knowledge and competence on an ongoing basis. In one important case, a nurse was found negligent after it was established that the nurse, who had worked in a physician's office in Alberta for 22 years, had failed to take any continuing education courses since the year after she had graduated, some 40 years before (*Dowey v Rothwell*, 1974).

Canadian Nurses Protective Society

A primary concern for nurses should be to maintain a high level of competence in nursing practice, excellent communication with clients, and awareness of the risks involved in performing nursing procedures. Nurses also must have some knowledge of the law, legal processes, the judicial system, the rights of their clients, and their own responsibilities. The Canadian Nurses Protective Society (CNPS) was established by the Canadian Nurses Association in 1988. Up to this time, the provincial/territorial nursing associations had contracted with insurance firms for professional liability insurance, which members obtained as a component of their membership in these associations. Associations perceived a need to develop an organization managed by the profession to minimize escalating costs of obtaining professional liability insurance on a province-by-province basis through insurance firms. The CNPS is a nonprofit organization offering professional liability insurance; this insurance is purchased by 10 of the 12 provincial/territorial associations on behalf of their members (all provincial/territorial associations except British Columbia and Quebec). The CNPS offers advice about professional liability to nurses from 0845 to 1630 hours Monday through Friday EST. Nurses may call CNPS about any situation with ethical/legal implications in which they have personal involvement or knowledge by calling a toll-free telephone number (1-800-267-3390) outside Ottawa or 237-2133 in Ottawa. Nurses may speak with a nurse-lawyer who will give immediate advice and assistance about steps to take in documenting an unusual occurrence and in understanding legal processes, and may refer nurses to experienced legal counsel.

■ Ethical Dilemmas in Health Care

Do Not Resuscitate Orders

Practising nurses are keenly aware of the ethical dilemmas they face in relation to "do not resuscitate" (DNR) or "no code" orders. If there is no written DNR order and a patient arrests, is the nurse expected to "code" the patient? Who is, or should be, involved in making such a decision? Are there, or should there be, differences in DNR policies in long-term care institutions versus acute-care settings?

A joint effort of the Canadian Medical Association (CMA), Canadian Nurses Association (CNA), Canadian Hospital Association (CHA), and Canadian Bar Association (CBA) has resulted in a "Joint Statement on Terminal Illness" published in *The Canadian Nurse* (1984). The guidelines have been used in formulating policy and procedure for institutions; however, they address only patients who are terminally ill and do not address such issues as chronic illness and age. Toth (1991, p. 5) states unequivocally that CPR should not be performed "on a patient for whom such an intervention would prolong the dying process rather than extend life," and that "strong consideration should be given to a policy that would make CPR the exception rather than the rule in long-term care institutions." The University of Alberta Hospitals' policy for "No CPR Order" reflects Toth's thinking in its rationale, stating: "CPR should not be attempted in cases in which such an intervention is not in the best interests of the patient. CPR performed for inappropriate indications may prolong the dying process rather then extend life and may lead to futile suffering of patients" (August 12, 1991). The rationale states further that health-care professionals are responsible for keeping informed about research findings "following attempted CPR in different age groups and disease states" so that their decisions about CPR are research-based. Although the physician is responsible for writing a DNR order and also conveying its meaning to the nursing staff, the nursing profession should contribute to the development of such guidelines. Davis and Aroskar (1983, p. 149) point out that "nurses are in a key position to notify the physician if the patient's condition changes, which change would indicate that the orders may need reassessment." This reinforces the need for careful nursing assessment and clear communication with physicians and the need for flexibility and wise judgment in applying orders based on changes in the patient's condition.

The policy indicates the importance of discussing the DNR order with the patient, guardian, and family and also recording this discussion in the progress notes; however, the literature raises questions about the extent to which patients are involved in such decisions. In a study of older adults in an acute-care and long-term care setting, Godkin (1992) found that most of the patients had limited knowledge of CPR and its possible outcomes, and that this knowledge was gained primarily through television, in which most of the attempts to resuscitate were successful. The majority had not discussed the question of CPR with a physician, and most had not discussed their wishes regarding care with anyone. Nonetheless, if given an opportunity, 85% would have chosen to be involved in deciding whether to have CPR, and 75% "hoped that their physician would inform them if they thought that CPR would be of no benefit to them" (Godkin, 1992, p. 114). Most of the patients favoured a collaborative approach to decisions about CPR, involving physicians, themselves, nurses, and family members. Most DNR policies in hospitals pertain only to terminally ill patients. Godkin (1992) suggests that such policies be made known so that every individual understands that current policy requires that CPR be performed on all non–terminally ill patients unless a DNR order is recorded on the chart. This would require that hospitals address the issue, to reduce the dilemmas faced by families and staff regarding CPR, reduce costs of giving CPR that was not desired by the patients, and prevent the situation of patients being unable to participate in the decision by the time a discussion is initiated.

Although both nurses and physicians value autonomous decision-making by patients, recent research shows that frequently the patient is not involved in the decision where participation is possible (Bedell and Delbanco, 1984; Bedell, Pelle, Maher, and Cleary, 1986; Evans and Brody, 1985; Savage, Cullen, Kirchhoff, Pugh, and Foreman, 1987). Bedell and Delbanco (1984) surveyed 154 physicians whose patients had been resuscitated and found that only 19% of the patients had discussed resuscitation with the physician before cardiac arrest occurred. They also found that 33% of the families had been consulted about resuscitation beforehand, but patients' competency to be involved in the decision had not been addressed. Youngner (1987) suggests some possible reasons physicians may not discuss resuscitation with their patients: lack of awareness, time pressure, discomfort about discussing such matters, and/or the paternalistic attitude of doing what the physician thinks is best for the patient. Such reactions fail to support the patient's right to self-determination and autonomy.

In a study of DNR policies and end-of-life decisions in acute-care settings in Alberta, Wilson (1993) found that 73% of the 135 accredited health-care facilities had a written DNR policy. Most had been developed in the 1990s to optimize decision-making and involve the patient in the process; however, these purposes had not been achieved in general. Detailed surveys of four of the facilities showed that DNR policies were not commonly followed and that almost one third of the time they were not implemented at all. Problems generally arose from late decision-making that excluded the patient from end-of-life decisions. Thus DNR policies seem to have limited effect on practice. Wilson (1993) identifies the need for internal assessment to measure nurses' and physicians' knowledge about the DNR policy. Further, she believes that if the policy is retained, adherence should be emphasized because "lack of adherence to organizational policy places health-care facilities in legal and ethical jeopardy" (p. 127). She suggests additional education about policies and perhaps designating a separate DNR chart form to improve recording and help to guide decision-making about DNR.

Wilson (1993) also found that no-CPR decisions usually were made late and thus did not create an ethical or legal dilemma for health professionals or family members "as everything possible appeared to have been done to restore health and prevent death" (p. 129). She noted that it was common practice for health professionals to use at least one life-sustaining technology, such as oxygen and/or intravenous therapy, to promote comfort during the end-stage dying process. Questioning whether comfort was always the outcome, Wilson (1993) identifies the need for research to determine whether such measures promote comfort or just extend the dying process.

Yarling and McElmurry (1983) propose authorizing both the responsible physician and the responsible nurse to write DNR orders, depending on the situation. Although this may seem like an onerous responsibility for the nurse, is it any greater than having to perform CPR when the nurse knows that the patient does not want it? Although nurses are unlikely to be granted such a privilege, it is important that nurses and physicians have mechanisms to discuss such questions and differences of opinion. In addition, patients must have the opportunity to participate in making such profound decisions before the critical occurrence, such as through advance directives.

Advance Directives

In recent years much attention has been given to developing advance directives to serve as guidelines for health practitioners and family members when an individual is no longer capable of making decisions. A report, *Advance Directives and Substitute Decision-Making in Personal Care*, published in March 1993 by the Alberta Law Reform Institute and the Health Law Institute, recommends that:

> legislation be introduced to enable individuals to execute a health-care directive, in which they can (1) appoint someone as their health-care agent, who will have authority to make health-care decisions on their behalf in the event of their being incapable of making those decisions personally; (2) identify anyone whom they do not wish to act as their health care proxy; and (3) provide instructions and information concerning future health-care decisions (Alberta Law Reform Institute, March 1993, p. 94).

Similar legal developments have taken place, or are in process, in Manitoba, Ontario, Newfoundland, British Columbia, and Saskatchewan. Storch and Dossetor (1994) found overwhelming support for the concept of advance health-care directives in a survey of Edmonton residents. Similarly, strong support for directives was found by Hughes and Singer (1992) in their survey of 1000 family physicians in Ontario; however, their findings also revealed that most respondents rarely discuss the idea with their patients.

Advance directives may be prepared in the form of a living will that enables individuals to state in advance whether they want "heroic or extraordinary measures" in the event they are unable to make known their wishes. This approach was rejected by the Alberta Law Reform Institute and Health Law Institute because of problems of interpretation with the use of such vague terms as "heroic" and "extraordinary" measures. For example, do they refer to CPR only, or do they include tube feeding and other measures designed to prolong life? They also rejected the endurable power of attorney approach, which "enables an individual, while mentally competent, to appoint someone who will have the authority to make health-care decisions on the donor's behalf once the donor becomes mentally incapable of making these decisions" (Alberta Law Reform Institute, 1993, p. 7). Rather, their approach is to legalize the concept of health-care directives so individuals can have control over who will make decisions on their behalf when they are unable to do so, and also have some control over the content of decisions by including specific instruction in the directive, if desired.

If advance directives are enacted by the Alberta legislature, Wilson (1993) emphasizes the need for health-care facilities to review, and perhaps revise, their DNR policy to change the method in which life-support preferences are determined and used in decision-making about care. Even if such legislation is not enacted, Wilson's findings reveal a need for action to enhance patient self-determination.

Flarey (1991, p. 19) identifies three major advantages in the use of advance directives: (1) to ensure that one's predetermined wishes are followed; (2) to help family members in making complex decisions; and (3) to guide health professionals regarding the individual's wishes in such circumstances. Despite these advantages, the use of advance directives will depend on the extent to which health-care agencies develop and implement such policies and ask patients whether they have developed an advance directive. Nurses can play an important role in ensuring that these goals are attained in their work settings by gaining representation on ethics committees and other policy-making bodies on advance directives, and by educating colleagues and the public about individual rights to self-determination.

Issues in Childbearing

A major ethical issue pertaining to child bearing is abortion. The issue is "the status of the fetus as a member of the human species when the existence of the fetus poses a threat to the physical, psychological, or social well-being of a pregnant woman and/or other family members" (Curtin, 1982, p. 240). Antiabortionists claim that the personhood of the fetus is being denied, whereas proabortionists maintain that the woman's right to self-determination cannot be denied. The latter emphasizes the burden imposed on society by an unwanted pregnancy and the future welfare of the child. Between the two extremes are those who favour abortions depending on circumstances surrounding the pregnancy, such as rape and incest.

The question of abortion may present problems for the individual nurse who is expected to participate in the care of patients having an abortion. The nurse is responsible, legally and morally, for ensuring that patients' needs are met and that patients are not neglected because of differing values (Curtin, 1982). Nurses must know the agency's policies about such participation before accepting a position. Health-care agencies must have clearly defined policies that they can communicate to potential employees and use when an ethical dilemma confronts staff members.

These policies have been challenged many times. For example, a decision of the Supreme Court of Canada made in 1988 endorses women's rights to self-determination in relation to abortion. Bill C43, passed in 1990 by the House of Commons, would permit abortion only if a continued pregnancy would jeopardize the woman's physical or mental health, as diagnosed by one physician only. Physicians were adamantly opposed to this change because of the possibility of criminal charges against them and because they would be required to provide pre-abortion and postabortion counseling. However, Bill C43 and other challenges have not been upheld, so the Supreme Court decision has prevailed.

Allocation of Health-Care Resources and Rationing of Health Care

Ethical issues in the allocation of health-care resources may be encountered at several levels. At the government level, public policies determine the type of health care that can be provided. Nurses and other health professionals have a responsibility to exercise their prerogatives and communicate with legislators to influence these policies. For example, as a result of a government's decision not to require seat belt use by law, a considerable portion of the health-care dollar is spent on people involved in automobile accidents.

Policies that influence the use of health-care resources also have been established at the institutional level. Too often, nurses have little influence on such policies, and they need to take action to affect decision-making and priority-setting. Decisions to develop programs often are made without adequate consideration of the implications to nursing practice; medical programs, such as heart transplants and joint replacements, have a great effect on the need for nursing care and could affect nurses' ability to respond to the demands placed on them. At the unit level, nurses must delineate problems that result from new programs and provide data that will permit a reasoned decision, although values and emotions often enter into these decisions. Fortunately, nurses have become more vocal in expressing their concerns and in providing facts that can influence decision-making, rather then merely responding to the decisions made by the physicians and hospital administrators.

Is it ethically and morally right to support activities that may jeopardize the patient or result in unequal or unfair distribution of resources among different programs within a health-care institution? Who determines the priorities in allocating resources, and what facts are considered? With the increasing proportion of older people in Canada and other developed countries, greater age may result in a smaller share of resources, even with the lobbying power seniors have developed. Many disadvantaged groups, such as the physically and mentally handicapped, the poor, and ethnic minorities, also may be exploited by such decisions.

Other factors that influence the allocation of resources in health-care legislation include consumer unrest and the patients' rights movement. Davis and Aroskar (1983, p. 26) believe that "health care policy cannot be the monopoly of providers any more than scientists should have the only say on biomedical research." Reasons for such a position are possible conflicts of interest, the large amount of taxes used to provide health care, nonmedical dimensions of health problems that may be critical factors, and the fact that "individual liberty and autonomy extend not only into the political arena but also into health care" (Davis and Aroskar, 1983, p. 206). Although nurses individually and collectively have gained greater influence on public policy through lobbying and working effectively with consumers and providers of care, they must increase their involvement. In addition to responding to particular issues, the professional organizations can work to influence public allocation of health-care resources.

Expenditures for health care as a percentage of Gross Domestic Product have been slowly rising over the past 4 decades since the advent of national health insurance in 1957. The practice of deficit budgeting adopted by the federal government in the 1970s and by provincial governments in the 1980s led by 1994 to large accumulated debt attributable to provincial and national governments. At 9.9% of Gross Domestic Product in 1991, national expenditures for health care became obvious targets for cuts and reductions in health programs (Health Canada, 1994). In such a climate, all health expenditures are being scrutinized, and governments are increasingly slashing spending in all areas. However, the legacy of federal government failure to defend the provisions of the Canada Health Act since 1984 and escalating expenditures for health at the provincial and federal levels have led to a questioning of the viability of the five basic principles of the Canada Health Act. Within certain provinces, facility fees for payments to physicians for services received in private health-care establishments have been permitted, thus undermining the public administration principle and the prohibition against user fee charges by the Canada Health Act. However, the imposition of an October15, 1995 deadline by the federal Minister of Health, Diane Marleau, for elimination of the facility fees being charged by the private clinics as a contravention of the Canada Health Act would indicate that the Liberal government in power intends to preserve the integrity of Medicare. Because Alberta was the biggest offender in allowing facility fees, its actions were of considerable interest. Indications from the Alberta government early in October, 1995 were that it planned to comply with the federal deadline in order to avoid the huge financial penalties that would be imposed if it failed to do so, even though it was seeking alternate ways of funding the private clinics.

Although there has always been rationing of health care in the Canadian health system, it has not been systematically applied. For some time, health-care agencies have used criteria for the admission of clients to certain treatment programs, such as kidney, heart, and liver transplant programs, primarily because the costs of such services are high, and the agencies are obliged to use resources in the most appropriate manner to benefit citizens. Some health professionals may have failed to fully inform clients about treatment options, believing that the course of action they suggested is the most important in the particular situation. In a society where health-care consumers are more knowledgeable and where the professional has an ethical and legal duty to explain all possible treatment and care to clients and their families, society is focusing more attention on the need to make rational choices about the provision of care, balanced by reasonable access to comprehensive care on a universal basis for all qualified residents of Canada. In other areas, physicians, nurses, and other health professionals have found themselves prolonging death rather than preserving life, and society is trying to come to grips with some of these situations. Models of care rationing in the public system of Medicare for those over 65 years of age in the United States are increasingly being evaluated in Canada for their applicability to the Canadian context. Issues in rationing of care are likely to continue over the next decade as the health system undergoes major restructuring and reform.

■ Strategies for Addressing Ethical Dilemmas in Practice

The number and variety of ethical dilemmas that nurses encounter in practice have increased because of advances in scientific knowledge and technologies. Nurses and physicians often become embroiled in ethical dilemmas in which opinions differ, leading to decreased communication and failure to work together in the interest of patients. These results can be detrimental to patient care and to the mental health and well-being of nursing staff, particularly in intensive care units, where nurses and physicians may disagree on life-and-death decisions, on approaches to care, and on priorities.

Some health-care agencies address these dilemmas through an ethics committee, which is called on an ad hoc basis to address dilemmas presented by nurses or physicians. In some large teaching hospitals, an ethicist is employed to provide expert assistance and guidance. At Montreal General Hospital, Dr. David Roy, an internationally renowned physician-ethicist, has helped nursing and medical staff address complex issues for many years. Institutional ethics committees are not a new venture in Canadian hospitals. The Canadian Hospital Association issued a policy statement recommending them in 1966. Avard, Griener, and Langstaff (1985) conducted a survey to determine their frequency, composition, and modus operandi. Their findings revealed great variability in size, composition, and function and that they were primarily advisory; however, the survey did not determine the effectiveness of the committees. A second survey by Storch and Griener (1990) was designed to determine the effectiveness of committees in addressing the ethical problem in self-determination. The data revealed that the status of ethics committees in Canadian hospitals was very similar in 1994 to what it was in 1989. The most evident change was an increase from 18% to 58.3% in the hospitals that had an ethics committee. Most respondents reported that the committees serve primarily in an advisory capacity; however, the survey did not determine whether such advice must be followed. To seek an answer to this question and others regarding the effectiveness of committees, a second phase of the study was undertaken through site visits to five selected hospitals for detailed review; the findings have not been reported to date.

A preventive strategy is designed to improve the teaching of ethics in nursing education by ensuring that ethics are an official part of the nursing curricula on the undergraduate and graduate levels and are taught by experts, not left to chance to be integrated into all teaching. Thompson and Thompson (1989) are advocates of this approach. They identify the goals of teaching ethics to professional students and professionals as: "to stimulate the moral imagination; recognize ethical issues; elicit a sense of moral obligation; develop analytical skills; and tolerate and reduce disagreements and ambiguity" (1989, p. 86). They recommend using case studies, as do many textbooks on ethics; however, expert guidance must be available during the process of analyzing the ethical issues and dilemmas presented.

Because many practising nurses who face ethical dilemmas every day have not received this education, a discussion of ethics should be included in inservice education and continuing education. After nurses have learned the theoretical foundation of ethics, ongoing bioethics rounds can be organized for nurses and physicians. Bioethics rounds are intended not to address ethical issues encountered in the care of a specific patient, but to provide opportunities for open discussion of ethical issues when the professionals involved can consider various viewpoints and do not face a specific ethical issue requiring an immediate decision. This approach has been in development through the Bioethics Centre since 1987 by the University of Alberta and the University of Alberta Hospitals. The project, a result of a collaborative effort to address ethical dilemmas, has equal representation from medicine, nursing, and philosophy through directors who plan and conduct bioethics rounds and who are responsible for joint teaching in ethics for nursing and medical students. Such a collaborative approach helps professionals address issues involving both professions so they are deliberated together and collaborative decisions are reached that are in the best interests of the patients and health-care providers. This approach is based on the belief that collaboration in the delivery of health care is required to address complex ethical dilemmas; there are no right or wrong answers, but decisions must be made that will meet the needs of the consumers of health care.

In this chapter, several legal and ethical questions have been discussed. Many more are addressed in books and journals for health professionals. The amount of literature on ethics has increased phenomenally in the past two decades, helping health professionals identify actions to take in practice situations. Although there are no easy answers to ethical or legal questions, health professionals must have access to resources in the literature and through ethicists and legal experts, and they must use these resources in dealing with complex issues and dilemmas.

■ REFERENCES

Alberta Law Reform Institute. (1993). *Advance directives and substitute decision-making in personal health care.* A joint report of the Alberta Law Reform Institute and the Health Law Institute, Report No. 64, Edmonton, Alberta.

Ares v Venner. (1970). S.C.R., 14, D.L.R. (3d) 4 (S.C.C.), p. 608.

Avard, D., Griener, G., & Langstaff, J. (1985). Hospital ethics committees: Survey reveals characteristics. *Dimensions, 62*(2), 24-26.

Bedell, S. & Delbanco, T. (1984). Choices about cardiopulmonary resuscitation in the hospital. *New England Journal of Medicine, 300,* 310-317.

Bedell, S., Pelle, D., Maher, L., & Cleary, P. (1986). Do not resuscitate orders of critically ill patients in the hospital. *Journal of the American Medical Association, 256,* 2.

Benjamin, M. & Curtis, Jr. (1986). *Ethics in nursing* (ed. 2). New York: Oxford University Press.

Brody, H. (1976). *Ethical decisions in medicine.* Boston: Little, Brown & Company.

Canadian Nurses Association. (1991). *Code of Ethics for Nursing.* Ottawa: The Association.

Canadian Nurses Association, Canadian Medical Association, and Canadian Hospital Association. (1984). Joint statement on terminal illness: A protocol for health professionals regarding resuscitative intervention for the terminally ill. *The Canadian Nurse, 80*(4), 24.

Curtin, L.L. (1982). Case study V: Abortion, privacy and conscience. In L. Curtin & M.J.Flaherty (Eds.), *Nursing ethics: theories and pragmatics,* (pp. 239-254). Bowie, MD: Robert J. Brady Company.

Curtin, L.L. (1985). Developing a professional ethic. *AARN Newsletter, 41*(10),1, 3-6.

Dais, E.E. (1973). Canadian law: an overview. In S.R. Good & J.C. Kerr (Eds.), *Contemporary issues in Canadian law for nurses* (pp. 3-14). Toronto: Holt, Rinehart & Winston.

Davis, A.J. & Aroskar, M.A. (1983). *Ethical dilemmas and nursing practice* (ed. 2). Norwalk, CT: Appleton-Century-Crofts.

Dowey v Rothwell (1974). 5 W.W.R. 311.

Duff, R.S. & Campbell, A.G.M. (1973). Moral and ethical dilemmas in the special-care nursery. *New England Journal of Medicine, 289,* 890-894.

Dyck, A.J. (1975). Beneficent euthanasia and benemortasia: Alternative view of mercy. In M. Kohl (Ed.), *Beneficent euthanasia* (pp. 120-126). Buffalo, NY: Prometheus.

Evans, A. & Brody, B. (1985). The do not resuscitate order in teaching hospitals. *Journal of the American Medical Association, 253,* 15.

Flarey, D. (1991). Advanced directives: In search of self-determination. *Journal of Nursing Administration, 21*(11), 16-22.

Francoeur, R.T. (1983). *Biomedical ethics: a guide to decision making.* Toronto: John Wiley & Sons.

Fry, S. (1992). Ethics and accountability: A report by Doreen Reid. *AARN Newsletter, 48*(7), 25-26.

Godkin, M.D. (1992). Cardiopulmonary resuscitation: Knowledge, attitudes and opinions of older adults in acute care and long-term care settings. Unpublished master's thesis, University of Alberta Faculty of Nursing, Edmonton.

Government of Canada. (1992). *The charter of rights and freedoms: a guide for Canadians.* Ottawa: Minister of Supply and Services Canada.

Grady, P.E. (1973). The law and nurses' notes. In S.R. Good & J.C. Kerr (Eds.), *Contemporary issues in Canadian law for nurses* (pp. 127-129). Toronto: Holt, Rinehart & Winston.

Health Canada. (1994). Preliminary estimates of health expenditures in Canada. *Provincial-territorial summary report, 1987-1991*. Ottawa: Health Information Division, Policy and Consultation Branch, Health Canada.

Hughes, D.L. & Singer, P.A. (1992). Family physicians' attitudes toward advance directives. *Canadian Medical Association Journal, 146*(11), 1937-1944.

International Council of Nurses. (1973). *ICN code for nurses—ethical concepts applied to nursing*, Geneva, Switzerland: International Council of Nurses.

Kluge, E.W. (1992). *Biomedical ethics in a Canadian context*. Toronto, ON: Prentice-Hall Canada, Inc.

McCormick, R.A. (1974). To save or let live: The dilemma of modern medicine. *Journal of the American Medical Association, 229*, 172-176.

Merryman, J.H. (1969). *The civil law tradition*. Palo Alto, CA: Stanford University Press.

Philpott, M. (1985). *Legal liability and the nursing process*. Toronto: W.B. Saunders.

Plucknett, T.F.T. (1956). *A concise history of the common law*. Boston: Little Brown & Co.

Robillard, H.M., High, D.M., Sebastian, J.G., Pisaneschi, J.I., Perritt, L.J., & Mahler, D.M. (1989). Ethical issues in primary care: A survey of practitioners' perceptions, *Journal of Community Health, 14*(1), 9-17.

Ross, M.W. (1973). The nurse as an employee. In S.R. Good & J.C. Kerr (Eds.), *Contemporary issues in Canadian law for nurses* (pp. 95-106). Toronto: Holt, Rinehart & Winston.

Savage, T., Cullen, D., Kirchhoff, K., Pugh, E., & Foreman, M. (1987). Nurses' response to do not resuscitate orders in the neonatal intensive care unit, *Nursing Research, 36*, 6.

Shaw, A. (1973). Dilemmas of "informed consent" in children. *New England Journal of Medicine, 289*, 885-890.

Storch, J.L. (1982). *Patients' rights: ethical and legal issues in health care and nursing*, Toronto: McGraw-Hill Ryerson.

Storch, J.L. & Griener, G. (June 1990). Ethics committees in Canadian hospitals: Report of 1989 survey. *The Bioethics Bulletin, 2*(2), 1-3. (Available from University of Alberta Division of Bioethics, Edmonton, Alberta.)

Storch, J.L. & Dossetor, J.B. (1994). Public attitudes toward end-of-life treatment decisions: Implications for nurse clinicians and nursing administrators. *Canadian Journal of Nursing Administration, 7*(3), 65-89.

Thompson, J.E. & Thompson, H.O. (1989). Teaching ethics to nursing students. *Nursing Outlook, 37*(2), 84-88.

Toth, E. (1991). Commentary on the national guidelines for no resuscitation orders. *The Bioethics Bulletin, 3*(3), 4-5. (Available from University of Alberta Division of Bioethics, Edmonton, Alberta.)

Wilson, D.M. (1993). The influences for do-not-resuscitate policies and end-of-life treatment or non-treatment decisions. Unpublished doctoral dissertation, University of Alberta, Edmonton.

Yarling, R. & McElmurry, B. (1983). Rethinking the nurse's role in do not resuscitate orders: A clinical policy proposal in nursing ethics. *Advances in Nursing Science, 5*(4), 1-12.

Youngner, S.J. (1987). DNR orders: No longer secret, but still a problem. *Hastings Center Report, 17*(1), 24-33.

3

THE SHAPE AND STRUCTURE OF HEALTH CARE IN CANADA

JANET ROSS KERR

The importance of health-care financing to society is reflected in the nature and quality of the service available, clients' eligibility for and access to health-care, and the affordability and accountability of the system. For health-care professionals, practice depends on the way the system is financed. In the case of nurses, the fact that they are primarily employees of health-care agencies means that as the quantity of health-care available in a publicly funded system is alternately expanded and withdrawn as a result of economic and political forces, the opportunity to practice also is subject to the uncertainties of resource allocation. This means that every professional group must fully understand and actively participate in the debate over financing arrangements. No subject is more controversial and more vital than the types of services to be provided, the choice of professional or occupational groups that will provide them, the determination of whether health care will be funded from public or private sources, and the form of remuneration for each group providing health care. Nurses must understand the issues in health-care financing and participate actively in the resolution of these issues both through their professional groups and as individuals (Ross Kerr, 1996).

■ Constitutional Responsibility for Health

The value placed upon life in contemporary society is reflected in arrangements to promote good health in the population and provide health care to those who require it. Under the terms of The British North America Act of 1867, responsibility for health was given to the provinces, a division of powers that was maintained in The Constitution Act of 1982. When the founding fathers decided to make health a provincial mandate, times were very different and health was not a priority of the fledgling colonial government. Because the era of remarkable scientific discoveries and concomitant advances in health knowledge had not yet begun, the importance of health in the next century and beyond would have been difficult to envision. The emergence of Canada as a progressive nation through the nurturing of its social democratic traditions from the colonial era, through the transition to full and independent partnership in the Commonwealth had major implications for societal perceptions of the necessity to offer health care on a just and equitable basis to all citizens.

■ The Evolution of Medicare

The initial attempts to develop prepaid medical and hospital insurance were born of war, depression, and social upheaval. The original plan for prepaid healthcare began ". . . in the early years of World War I when rural municipalities in Saskatchewan began to employ physicians on contract to provide general practitioner services through local property taxes and 'premiums' for non-property owners" (Taylor, 1980, p. 184). Plans to prepay hospital services developed in conjunction with the municipal doctor program and "by 1939, about 100 municipal plans were operating" in Saskatchewan (p. 184). The heartbreaking suffering of people who could not afford health care gave leaders such as Premier Tommy Douglas in Saskatchewan the motivation to work to make health care a service financed by the system of taxation. As a child, Douglas had suffered from osteomyelitis in one of his legs. The standard treatment of the day was amputation, but Douglas was identified from his standard ward hospital bed as an interesting candidate for a new procedure to remove the infected part of the bone by a visiting private surgeon. He was offered the surgery, not because he was deserving, but because a demonstration of the procedure was considered important for the teaching of medical students. Thus, instead of going through life as an amputee, Tommy Douglas was given a new lease on life, and he became a middle weight boxing champion and later, premier of Saskatchewan. His experience clearly shaped Douglas' thinking about the structure and financing of health care, and he said many years later in the legislature of Saskatchewan that he became committed to equal access to health care at an early age. Advocating a national health insurance scheme required a fundamental shift from thinking about health care as a privilege to health care as a right and was as controversial in the early decades of the twentieth century as it is today. The fact that Saskatchewan became the first area of the country to pass legislation allowing municipalities to raise taxes to support the employment of physicians, the establishment of hospitals, and the development of hospital and medical insurance plans is important because the province was perhaps the region of the country most deeply affected by the poverty accompanying the

Depression. In the forefront of health-care financing in the country, the Saskatchewan model would influence the federal government to introduce a health-care financing package offering universal access to health care to all residents, including all provinces by 1971. The experience with prepaid hospital and medical care in Saskatchewan provided the springboard for the passage of legislation in 1947 establishing the first compulsory hospital insurance plan in North America by the Cooperative Commonwealth Federation party, the party first elected 3 years earlier under Douglas' leadership.

The National Health Grants Act of 1968

In 1945 the federal government had developed a plan for national health insurance, but despite public support, the federal offer was rejected by the wealthiest provinces and the initiative collapsed. Instead, in the last year of Prime Minister Mackenzie King's term, his Liberal government introduced the National Health Grants Act, legislation that provided financing for hospital construction and was comparable in many ways to the Hill-Burton Act in the United States. Because of the lack of progress at the federal level, in 1949 British Columbia and Alberta developed their own compulsory hospital insurance plans. Also in 1949, Newfoundland with its publicly administered cottage hospital system, joined the Confederation. Thus another province was committed to national health insurance. The four provinces already committed to a national plan were augmented in 1955 by Ontario, which "joined these four in pressuring the federal government to honour at least the hospital benefit stage of its 1945 health insurance offer" (Taylor, 1980, p.187). With a large proportion of the Canadian population in five provinces on board, the federal government at last had the mandate to enact its proposals.

The Hospital Insurance and Diagnostic Services Act of 1957

Thus the passage of the Hospital Insurance and Diagnostic Services Act in 1957 offered federal assistance to make "prepaid coverage universally available to all residents, including diagnostic services to in-hospital patients and a broad range of out-patient services" (Taylor, 1980, p. 189). The plan involved a 50-50 cost-sharing arrangement for inpatient and outpatient hospital services. Because of the constitutional power of the provinces in the area of health, each province had the opportunity to decide whether to join the national effort. However, because the plan involved 50-50 cost sharing, any province that chose not to join would forfeit its own tax dollars and effectively subsidize the plans operating in the other provinces. When the Act took effect in 1958, the five provinces that had expressed support for the national plan agreed to participate. However, by 1961 all provinces had agreed to do so. Excepted from the national hospital insurance program were tuberculosis hospitals, mental hospitals, and certain other health institutions. As a result of this program, Blue Cross plans and plans operated by insurance companies phased out coverage for a standard-ward hospital bed and shifted their focus to other hospital benefits that were not covered.

The Medical Care Insurance Act of 1966

Medical care was not a part of this health insurance coverage offered to the provinces. Although the General Council of the Canadian Medical Association had passed a resolution in January, 1943, endorsing the principle of health insurance, the expansion of the prepaid medical plans sponsored by the profession changed this policy in the early 1950s (Taylor, 1980, pp. 185, 187). Again Saskatchewan was to be the catalyst in the transition to prepaid medical insurance universally available to residents of Canada. The Douglas government knew that the development of prepaid hospital insurance was its most important legislative success, and it extended this insurance to cover physicians' services despite the vehement opposition of this powerful professional group. The ensuing physicians' strike in Saskatchewan was a bitter struggle that shocked the country and lasted 23 days. The parties compromised, with the provincial government allowing physicians to opt out of the plan and bill patients directly if they chose to do so, and the physicians conceding "to the government the right to enrol everyone and to determine benefit levels" (Taylor, 1980, p. 188). This led to the federal Medical Care Insurance Act of 1966, which expanded the system of prepaid hospital coverage to include medical care for all residents of Canada. The controversy over this legislation may explain the fact that only two provinces participated at the time the legislation became effective on July 1, 1968. However, the federal government undoubtedly took some of its cues from the Saskatchewan experience and allowed a 5-year period for all provinces to enter into a federal-provincial arrangement for the prepayment of medical services. The plan covered physicians' services in and out of hospital but did not prevent provinces from allowing physicians to opt out of the plan, bill patients directly, requiring them to seek reimbursement from the plan, or impose surcharges on the established fee for a particular service.

The Fiscal Arrangements and Established Programs Financing Act of 1977

Because health costs had escalated by the early 1970s and because health-care expenditures as a proportion of Gross Domestic Product were continuing to rise, the federal government was concerned about the open-ended or "blank cheque" approach of the 50-50 cost sharing arrangement of the hospital insurance act. The passage of the Fiscal Arrangements and Established Programs Financing Act in 1977 replaced 50-50 cost sharing with block funding. The latter involved transfer of some tax points to the provinces and reduced the federal contribution to health care to 25%. Additional federal contributions were based on increases in Gross Domestic Product. Dissatisfied with the fee schedule negotiated between their professional group and the provincial government in the late 1970s, physicians increasingly used copayments or extrabilling to ensure that fees for various services were as high as they believed they should be. Members of the public voiced a similar concern about another form of copayment, called user fees, for various forms of institutional services.

The Canada Health Act of 1984

To address its concerns about the erosion of medicare, the federal government passed The Canada Health Act of 1984. Under its provisions, extrabilling and user fees were disallowed, and a new clause was added to allow federal reimbursement for the services of "health practitioners" in addition to physicians and dental surgeons. This provision opened the door for nurse practitioners to be used to provide a broad range of primary health-care services, where funding for these had formerly been restricted to physicians. Although physicians were strongly opposed to the passage of legislation that would disallow extrabilling, the Act was passed by the Liberal government of Pierre Elliott Trudeau. The enduring popularity of Medicare is reflected in the fact that a new Progressive Conservative government elected in 1984 did not make any move to amend the legislation or to develop new proposals, even though it was lukewarm to national health insurance.

Facility Fees and the Impending Loss of Federal Funding for Medicare

Elected in 1984, the Mulroney government downplayed the Canada Health Act over its 8 years in power by reducing federal contributions to provincial health-care plans and by allowing provinces to permit payment of "facility fees" by patients to physicians who performed surgical and other procedures in specially equipped suites and clinics in their offices. As the federal government turned a blind eye to the provisions of the Canada Health Act, physicians again were permitted to extrabill or charge the patient directly over and above what the provincial plan paid for physicians' services. An amendment to the Federal-Provincial Fiscal Arrangements Act and Federal Postsecondary Education and Health Contribution Act by the progressive conservative govenment of Prime Minister Brian Mulroney identified certain sequential targets for reducing and eventually eliminating deficit spending and would have had the effect of reducing federal government contributions to health care on a rigid schedule until the federal share was eliminated entirely. At this point, the Canada Health Act no longer would carry any weight with the provinces because of the federal government's lack of jurisdiction over health care under the Constitution. Any power wielded by the federal government in health care has strictly depended on its role in financing provincial health plans, and the old adage "he who pays the piper calls the tune" applies here. The Liberal government of Jean Chrétien, elected in 1993, weighed its courses of action carefully in the first 2 years of its mandate and also passed an amendment to the above two federal acts that was assented to on March 24, 1994. The effect of this amendment was to extend the timetable for the gradual reduction of federal contributions to the provinces for health to March 31, 1999. This piece of legislation was a disappointment to many because it did not appear to maintain a relatively high level of federal contributions to health care, thereby no longer ensuring that provincial plans upheld federal standards through the financing of provincial plans. However, on January 6, 1995, federal Minister of Health, Diane Marleau, gave the provinces an October 15, 1995 deadline to prohibit private clinics from charging facility fees while the physicians practising in them were paid fees for their services through public monies from Medicare. The penalty of fines on a dollar for dollar basis would amount to billions in the provinces continuing to allow facility fees beyond the deadline. The reason given by the Minister for her decision was that restricting access to the private clinics to those who could afford treatment contravened the terms of the Canada Health Act. After protesting loudly to the federal government about this ruling, Alberta, the province in which the use of facility fees was the most widespread, announced in early October 1995 that it would comply with the deadline. The integrity of the Canada Health Act is still under attack, and whether the highly popular system of national health insurance will survive in Canada remains to be seen.

■ The Philosophical Basis of Medicare

National health insurance always has been a popular program of provincial and federal governments, and Canadians have come to believe passionately in their right to health care supported by a system of health insurance. However, a task force of the Canadian Bar Association examined whether Canadians have a legal right to health care, and concluded that "there is no right to health care under the *Charter of Rights and Freedoms.*" The exception to this was the province of Quebec, which passed legislation articulating the right to health care within certain parameters and as such represents "an innovative and useful model" for other provinces to consider (Canadian Bar Association, 1994, p. 37). However, the report also stated that "Notwithstanding the above, there is a general expectation among the Canadian public that there is a right to health care. As a result, there is a gap between the lack of a right to health care and the expectation by the public" (Canadian Bar Association, 1994, p. 26).

At the foundation of the national health insurance system are the five basic principles of health care, from which standards for the legislation are derived. The first principle, *universality*, refers to coverage offered to the population as a whole rather than to selected population groups. Therefore coverage is extended to all qualified residents. The principle of *comprehensiveness* ensures that all medically necessary services included in the plan are covered. Although at the outset extra-billing and user fees were permitted, since the passage of the Canada Health Act of 1984, such charges may not be applied for services that are covered by the plan. *Accessibility* of health care may be the most difficult to assure, in that Canada's population is relatively sparse and spread over a vast territory. Reasonable access to medically necessary services is seen as essential, despite geographic and transportation difficulties. *Portability* or coverage for residents of a province who require health services just after a move or during a visit to another province is assured in plans, although some difficulties have resulted from differences between fees in provinces and in obtaining full reimbursement from the home province. *Public administration* or nonprofit administration of services by an organization fiscally responsible to the provincial government also is required. Since 1957, the standards based on these five principles, and with which the provincial plans must comply to receive federal funding, have been fine-tuned.

The philosophical basis for the development of the Canadian system of national health insurance is rooted in humanitarian and social democratic traditions. In a society in which life is a deep and enduring value, the health of people becomes an issue of fundamental importance. Ensuring that access to needed care is available to the population as a whole, rather than to only those with enough money to buy the care they need, reflects this value of equality of citizens and the framework of social justice underlying the health-care system. Factors such as Canada's status as a colonial nation and major social upheavals of war and depression were undoubtedly significant in the system of health insurance that evolved. Such a system requires that taxes are assessed and pooled to provide health care to the population. Pursuit of the common good has led the electorate to support the collection of tax revenue earmarked for health care and managed by governments for the provision of health care services.

From the outset, the Canadian system of national health insurance developed in a fashion similar to systems in other Western countries. The fact that the provincial plans insure hospital care and care by physicians has meant dominant roles for hospitals and physicians in the system. The fact that the number of hospital beds increased at a rate much greater than the population until the 50-50 federal/provincial cost-sharing arrangement was ended is significant. Care centred in the home and community health services of various types were not eligible for federal cost-sharing in the initial legislation. The exclusion of community-based health services from federal financing encouraged physician-centred, in-hospital care during the first 35 years of health-care legislation in Canada (Ross Kerr, 1996). The high cost of in-hospital care, the use of physicians as "gatekeepers" to the health-care system, and the lack of health outcomes that were significantly better than other western

nations spending less on health-care led to a search for more effective, more efficient, and lower-cost alternatives. The "Alma Ata" agreement by countries that are
members of the World Health Organization of "health for all by the year 2000," has
challenged western nations to adopt a more community-focused approach with
meaningful community involvement and influence. Health-care reform is a slogan
now being heard across the country. Although this term means different things to
different people, there are some fundamental assumptions that the health-care system of the future will look quite different from that of today. Community-based
care will enhance and facilitate health maintenance, health promotion, and
prevention of disease, balancing these with measures to restore health:

> Many believe that it will not be possible to sustain the current system without major
> modifications. Task forces and commissions in most provinces are looking at ways to
> shift the heavy focus on physician and institutional care to "community based" alterna-
> tives and non-physician providers (Deber, Hastings, and Thompson, 1991, pp. 73-74).

■ Threats to Medicare

Threats to medicare are not new and show no signs of diminishing. The issues
are complex, interdependent, and consequential. One of the difficulties that has
been central to health-care reform across the country is the fact that the provinces
and the federal government have been running large deficits for a number of years.
As a consequence of this failure to balance budgets, provincial and federal debt
levels are so high that the interest costs of the debt have mounted to the point
where they are becoming insupportable. Appeals to voters to endorse drastic cuts
in government spending and services to eliminate deficit financing and to pay
down debt are increasingly being heard by a concerned populace. Because health
care is one area of high government spending, it is fast becoming the target of
intense budget slashing efforts. However, some are concerned about planning
when dollars are cut out of health budgets in the absence of an overall plan for
making the system more efficient. This lack of planning carries serious risks for
both the present and future. Because any plan reflects a fundamental philosophy
and principles, one is alarmed to see major cuts in health-care spending in the
absence of identification of the values and principles of the system and determining more effective ways for the system to function. Needed reforms with their
associated efficiencies also might not be implemented because of political pressure
applied by groups with vested interests.

The needs of professional groups must be balanced by the needs of society.
In the evolving health-care system in Canada, there is a need for collaboration
between professional groups. Up to now, the system has been such that governments attempted to cater to the demands of particular groups, when this may not
have benefitted clients or the system as a whole. Although achieving a consensus

on contentious issues may be difficult for professional groups, boards, and the public, they must work toward this goal and ensure that the voices of all interested parties are both heard and considered in the continuing debate over the shape and structure of health care. Governments are elected to act in the best interests of the people as a whole. Medicare is a highly popular program, but programs must change significantly to achieve efficiencies. At the same time, it is important to maintain the integrity of the system in providing a high standard of care to Canadians based on the basic principles fundamental to The Canada Health Act.

Limits to Available Resources

Limits to growth in the postindustrial society increasingly are being recognized in all sectors of human activity. In the expansionist decades of the 1950s and 1960s, many believed that no health-care expense was too much for the public purse to bear. From 1970 onward, it has become clear that consumption of health care will continue to rise unless the system is rationalized and made more efficient. The discussion is tempered by the fact that, despite skyrocketing expenses, the health status of the population has not increased at a corresponding rate. In fact, when Canada's health status is compared to other developed countries through recognized indices, there does not seem to have been a benefit to spending more than most of these other countries. Ways of helping the population as a whole to recognize and adopt healthy lifestyles will be an integral part of efforts to make the system more affordable by reducing the general impact and the high cost of preventable health problems. In rationalizing the system, it is important to identify health goals in Canadian society and fine tune the delivery system to support these. Limits to resources must be considered as part of the process of making the health-care system rational, because the system of the future must be supportable and sustainable.

Misuse of the System

Professionals and politicians often accuse health-care clients of misusing the system. This is tantamount to saying that members of the public are expected to understand the nature of a particular problem they are experiencing and how it should be solved. The health-care consumer would then consult the most appropriate professional provider in the proper setting for the particular problem. These expectations are terribly high and somewhat unrealistic. The practice of using emergency rooms for minor ailments rather than seeing physicians in their offices, medicentre locations, or primary health centres often is cited as an example of misuse of the system by consumers. Although some consumers realize that emergency room care is inappropriate for minor problems, others do not recognize this. The fact that hospital emergency rooms are available for minor complaints no doubt serves to reinforce the inappropriate use of this service.

The misuse of the system also is affected by the false assumption that misuse is client-driven. In many cases, "misuse" is provider-driven and routine. Examples are unnecessary follow-up visits to physicians or directions by the physician to come to the emergency room, where it is more convenient for the physician to provide care. Roos (1992) has identified geographic areas where high rates of particular types of surgery can be mapped. These are clearly provider-generated and undoubtedly represent misuse of the system. Even annual physical examinations are being questioned as unnecessary and costly to the health-care system, despite the fact that the population has been taught that these examinations are essential to health promotion and disease prevention. Whether the population can be persuaded to forgo yearly physical examinations is not known. However, if physicians and nurses are used more efficiently in the system, much more than this may be possible.

Maldistribution of Physicians

The maldistribution of physicians across the country in the face of an over-supply of these highly trained professionals is a recognized problem. However, few solutions have emerged. Physicians historically have been reluctant to locate their practices in areas remote from large urban centres. This is also true of other health professionals, but the independence of physicians with their private practices means that they have more control over where they will live and work. Because physicians are reimbursed for their services on a fee-for-service basis subject to terms and conditions placed on the fee schedule under provincial health plans, provincial governments have attempted to influence where physicians practise by a number of means. One such attempt was challenged in a lawsuit in British Columbia after the province implemented a system of assigning billing numbers for the number of physicians deemed necessary for each location in the province, thus limiting the number of physicians who could bill the health-care plan for services and therefore the supply of physicians. The Supreme Court of British Columbia upheld the physicians, and the province was barred from matching billing numbers with needs of communities and thereby restricting the supply of physicians. Since then, some provinces have instituted measures to control costs, such as capping the total amount available for medical services, capping the overall amounts physicians are allowed to bill the plan annually, and limiting the number of physicians who can move to a province and bill the plan for services. Changing the method of remunerating physicians from fee-for-service to salary or contract is being widely discussed. As provinces regionalize health services in a continuing quest for a more efficient and effective health-care system, finding a more cost-effective means of paying for physicians' services is likely to be high on the agenda.

Underutilization of Nurses

Nurses historically have been underutilized in the health-care system. This has resulted in part from the entrenchment of Medicare, beginning with legislation to provide funds for hospital construction in 1948 and continuing with hospital insurance legislation passed in 1957 and the prepaid medical insurance legislation of 1966. Physicians and hospitals have dominated health insurance legislation, and this has produced a focus on acute care and in-patient hospital treatment in health-care over the more than 40 years of federal financing of health care in Canada. From roles as private entrepreneurs in the early part of the century, nurses became employees in the health-care agencies that evolved after widespread unemployment during the Depression, while physicians continued to be private entrepreneurs, able to control the nature and size of their practices as well as the location in which they provided their services. Although nurses were employed largely by hospitals in the 30 years after World War II, the tremendous expansion in the number and size of hospitals resulted in a corresponding increase in the number of positions for registered nurses, even though nursing auxiliaries increasingly were employed in hospitals. In addition to the increase in demand for nurses, the roles of nurses have continually expanded in almost all areas of practice, especially in a variety of areas of specialized practice as a result of the great increases in technology and health knowledge.

Nursing education entered the university after World War I, when the demand for nurses with public health knowledge was first heard. From certificate programs in public health nursing, universities eventually developed undergraduate degree programs in nursing that incorporated a generalist knowledge of nursing, including public health and health assessment. Graduate programs at the master's level followed in the postwar expansionary period and concentrated on developing skills in advanced nursing practice and research. Doctoral programs in nursing have been established recently and have extended the range of preparation available in nursing. Nursing education has become more sophisticated over the past 2 decades, with an increased number of baccalaureate and master's degree students. Concomitantly, a greater proportion of all students entering nursing education are being admitted to programs offering a baccalaureate degree in nursing. Master's degree programs are available in all areas of the country and are admitting more students than previously, while the five doctoral programs in nursing are concentrated in British Columbia, Alberta, Ontario, and Quebec. In some provinces, the percentage of registered nurses prepared at the baccalaureate level is over 20%, and this figure is rising quickly.

Nurses are and have been receiving sophisticated preparation to meet the needs of a changing health-care system. However, their skills are not being used to their greatest advantage because of the entrenched physician and hospital domination of health care. In an environment where all assumptions on which service delivery is based are being questioned, nurses likely will be increasingly asked to use the full range of their skills to benefit the health-care consumer. As the focus of health care shifts to the community, nurses are in a unique position to serve the needs of clients because the degree programs that have prepared increasing numbers of nurses always have recognized the importance of community health nursing and have devoted a considerable amount of time to instruction in this area. In the shift to the community, nurses who have been prepared in diploma programs undoubtedly will require further preparation in community health to allow them to adapt to the health-care system of the future. More effective utilization of nurses will allow physicians to concentrate on areas of diagnosis and treatment that require their specialized expertise, and improved health-care outcomes and a more efficient and effective system are likely to result.

■ What Does the Future Hold?

The health-care system of the future is likely to look very different from its form of today and yesterday. The changes are rapid, extensive, and wide-ranging, covering virtually all areas of health care. The system of the future will incorporate principles of primary health care to a much greater extent than the system that has dominated to date in Canada. Consumers, who are considerably more knowledgeable today than their counterparts of yesteryear, will be much more informed and involved in decision-making about their health care. The efforts of health-care professionals will be directed increasingly toward educating consumers so that they can assume more responsibility for their own health. The community focus will produce cost-efficient community health centres. The first health professional a consumer will see in a nonemergent situation, however, likely will be a nurse rather than a physician, as physicians will no longer be the "gatekeepers" of the system. Home visits by home-care nurses will be common as consumers cope at home with conditions and treatments that previously would have meant a hospital stay. An integrated multidisciplinary focus will become a reality, with all health professionals working together for the interests of the client, rather than in an isolated fashion in different locations in the community. Social and cultural influences on health will require much study and attention to produce improved health outcomes. The political framework, within which the issues of health-care insurance plans are debated and determined, will be affected by the economic and social needs to fundamentally change the system. Decisions to move to a community-based model emphasizing disease prevention, promotion of health, and partnerships between professionals and consumers will be difficult, but ultimately hold the greatest potential for improving health. Issues of hospital governance, education of health professionals, integration of boards of health agencies on a regional basis, and restructuring of the systems for providing care and for remunerating health professionals in a reasonable and rational way must be considered in a collaborative manner to enable the health-care system in Canada to meet the challenges ahead in this century and beyond. The opportunity for better and less expensive health care as a result of the shifting focus of care is there, but whether the potential is realized remains to be seen.

■ REFERENCES

Canadian Bar Association. (1994). *What's law got to do with it?* Ottawa: The Association.

Deber, R.B., Hastings, J.E.F., & Thompson, G.G. (1991). Health-care in Canada: Current trends and issues. *Journal of Public Health Policy, 12*(1), pp. 72-82.

Roos, N.P. (1992). Hospitalization style of physicians in Manitoba: The disturbing lack of logic in medical practice. *Health Services Research, 27*(3), pp. 361-384.

Ross Kerr, J.C. (1996). The organization and financing of health-care. In J.C. Ross Kerr & J. MacPhail (Eds.), *Canadian nursing: issues and perspectives.* Toronto: Mosby–Year Book.

Taylor, M.G. (1980). The Canadian health insurance program. In C.A. Meilicke & J.L. Storch (Eds.), *Perspectives on Canadian health and social services policy: history and emerging trends* (pp. 181-219). Ann Arbor, MI: Health Administration Press.

4

Issues in the Care of Acutely Ill Adults and Children

Anita Molzahn

Acute illness refers to short-term episodic illness that requires diagnosis and short-term treatment. Adults and children who were acutely ill traditionally have been treated in hospitals. As a result, hospitals have been perceived as the centre of health care, providing the bulk of care to acutely ill adults and children. However, acute care increasingly is provided in the community. Although government and professional publications have stressed the importance of primary, preventive, and community-based health-care programs for some time, this shift to the community has resulted partly from rationing and reallocation of health-care funding.

Many new initiatives and programs have been developed to accomplish the goals of health-care reform. These programs are more participative than in the past and give people opportunities to make health decisions and care for themselves and their family members with support as needed from the community agencies and professionals. Some of these programs that relate to the care of acutely ill adults and children are described in this chapter. The issues include health care reform, the changing character of hospitals, acute care in the north, and ethical issues.

■ Health-Care Reform

Health-care reform is sweeping the country. In Canada, provinces are responsible for health care. The federal government provides some funding through transfer payments, but the proportion of funding for health care coming from the federal government is slowly decreasing and will disappear by 2007 (1997 in Quebec) (Kirby, 1992). Largely because health-care costs were rising at a time when tax revenues were declining, most provincial governments initiated major reviews of the health-care system, and reviewers have recommended significant changes to the health-care system.

In Canada, the term *health-care reform* has been characterized by reductions in the number of acute-care hospital beds, greater emphasis on health promotion and prevention of illness and injury, and greater participation of all affected parties in decision-making. The use of this term is distinctly different from the usage in the United States, where it has come to be equated with funding of health care.

Reductions in Acute-Care Hospital Beds

The British Columbia Royal Commission on Health Care and Costs (Seaton, et al., 1991) noted that about 25% of the acute-care days provided in 1989-1990 were not required. With the average costs of hospitalization in acute-care hospitals rising to $1000 per day, significant resources would be saved if community-based care rather than hospitalization was provided. Clearly there has been waste in the health-care system. Over the past few years, many hospitals have eliminated beds, largely to reduce costs of operation. Given the economic realities, downsizing or "rightsizing" (Collins & Noble, 1992) has become common. The number of beds that have been eliminated is difficult to determine, but apparently few hospitals have not closed beds and reduced staff numbers.

Efforts have been made to avoid duplication of services and to regionalize specialized care. For some specialized equipment and procedures (e.g., lithotripsy, CT scanners, MRI scanners, transplantation, open-heart surgery, dialysis), some have considered designating only one hospital in the community to provide the service. For example, in Victoria, all pediatric and obstetrical care has been moved to one hospital.

To reduce the costs of services and to attain economies of scale, hospitals around the country have been merging (Johnson, Coombs, and Wood, 1991). The Greater Victoria Hospital Society was one of the first hospital groups to accomplish this type of merger. Today the many other examples include the Toronto Hospital and the Caritas Health Group in Edmonton. These mergers provide opportunities to reduce administrative costs and to avoid duplication of services.

Another sign of the times is restructuring. Many large hospitals in Canada are reorganizing. The goal generally is to reduce the number of layers in the hierarchy (Monk and Edgar, 1991). In many settings, the reorganization provides the opportunity for change; in many cases, hospital staff are given opportunities to have greater input into decision-making through models such as shared governance (Perry and Code, 1991). Although the goals of these changes seem to be laudable, a more cynical observation may be that these changes are resulting from the scarcity of economic resources.

Concurrently with reductions in numbers of hospital beds, budget cutting, restructuring, and mergers, the number of nurses who have been laid off and are unemployed has risen dramatically. In Canada, 72% of nurses are employed by hospitals (O'Brien-Pallas, 1992). When hospitals cut costs, nurses usually are affected because a significant proportion of the hospital budget is allocated to units for nursing staff. The number of nurses receiving unemployment insurance benefits increased from 1876 in 1990 to 3742 in 1992. These figures do not fully represent the effect of job losses on nurses because unemployment insurance benefits can be collected for less than 1 year. Many nurses are underemployed, working part-time or casual hours when they would like to be working full-time. As well, many nurses have moved into other fields of employment; some have established independent practices. The opportunities for new graduates to practice are extremely limited. When the author surveyed nurses in clinical practice settings about the issues they face in their nursing practice, nurses seemed unable to focus on clinical issues. Rather, nurses are concerned about their own job security, and the effect of bed reductions and financial cutbacks on patient care.

With the attempts to reduce utilization of acute-care hospital beds, more ambulatory care, day surgery, home care, and outpatient services have been developed. This means that people who previously would have been hospitalized now receive care at home. Individuals who are admitted to hospitals are more acutely ill, have more complex nursing and medical care requirements, and have a shorter length of stay than ever before. Sara Jane Growe (1991) suggested that hospitals of the future will look like intensive care units do today. This trend presents nurses with new challenges.

Health Promotion and Disease Prevention

The focus of the health care reform movement on health promotion and disease prevention is vitally important. This focus was recommended by the Canadian Nurses Association in the 1988 document entitled *Health for All Canadians: A Call for Health Care Reform*. Many royal commissions and reports (including the Seaton Commission Report on Health Care and Costs in British Columbia and the Rainbow Report in Alberta) have recommended that health care shift from the hospital to the community. Nevertheless, the largest proportion of funding for health care in Canada still is devoted to curative and illness-focused care; 3% of the health budget is estimated to be allocated to health promotion and prevention of illness (New Directions, 1993).

Many people (including nurses, physicians, and the public) have said that reductions in funding to the hospital sector have not resulted in shifting of resources to the community. Support services to assist people to function in their own homes are not always available. One also must consider the direct and indirect costs of community-based care to families. Seaton et al. estimated that 70% to 80% of our health care is provided informally and voluntarily, largely by family members (1991). With the trend toward community-based care, this proportion is likely to increase. In the past, the costs of medications, equipment, supplies, and respite care were covered by hospitals. However, when people with acute illnesses receive care at home, resources are not always available to support the costs of the treatment. Indirect and social costs to families (such as loss of employment income) often are not considered. Greater efforts must be made to develop professional and nonprofessional support groups and respite programs that can alleviate family/caregiver stress (Irvine and Dreger, 1991). Reimbursement plans need to be considered for people who may be saving the health-care system many dollars, but who fall through the cracks because they have chosen community-based care.

Most people think that the place for health promotion is the community. However, there is considerable confusion regarding the meaning of health promotion; there is more to health promotion than considerations of life-style. Health promotion has been defined as "the process of enabling people to increase control over and improve their health. It focuses on the population as a whole in the context of everyday life rather than dealing with specific diseases. Health promotion works to influence the determinants of health, such as poverty, education, and the environment. It encourages public participation in improving the health of communities" (RNABC, 1990). Under this definition of health promotion, health promotion clearly is a part of nursing practice. This role is only likely to increase, given the current trends. Hospital nurses have developed close partnerships with clients and members of the community. With an expanded mandate and new resources, they can adopt a greater working role in health-promotion initiatives.

Interest is growing in hospitals as providers of health-promotion activities within the hospitals. The Victoria Health Project was one example of hospitals collaborating with the community on health-promotion efforts. Given the present size of the institutional sector, the shifts in the focus can result in major contributions to health promotion.

Greater Participation in Decision Making

The third element in health care reform has been the involvement of clients in decision making. Over the last 30 or more years, individuals have been given more choices in their treatment and care. The right of clients to self-determination has become well-entrenched in health care. Hospital staff also are being given more opportunities to become involved in decisions relating to their work. Many agencies have implemented shared governance models to give staff these opportunities.

This has given nurses opportunities to contribute to decisions about patient care, freedom to collaborate with other professionals, and involvement in committees with mandates relating to nursing practice (Perry and Code, 1991).

In British Columbia, the Royal Commission on Health Care and Costs (Seaton, et al., 1991), has shifted authority for planning and coordinating local health services from the Ministry of Health to community health councils and regional health boards. Both professionals and members of the public were appointed to these councils and boards. A Provincial Health Council was appointed to establish provincial health goals, to develop means of measuring success in attaining these health goals, to promote public awareness about health issues, and to report to the public.

These trends in health care are consistent with society's focus on "empowerment." Patients and health-care professionals often feel powerless in large institutions such as hospitals. "Empowerment describes our intentional efforts to create more equitable (fair) relationships with one another, relationships in which there is greater equality in resources, status and authority" (RNABC, 1992). Through a range of strategies, including personal empowerment, small group development, community organization, coalition advocacy, and political action, individual clients and health-care professionals are becoming more involved in decision making in areas that affect them personally and health care in the community around them.

■ Changing Character of Hospitals

Hospitals in Canada are different from hospitals in the United States. Although the care is of comparable quality and the procedures and technologies are very similar, the reimbursement system has presented nurses with different challenges. Nurses in Canada are not required to collect detailed information about the supplies and equipment they use for charge backs; theoretically this enables them to spend more time with clients than with administrative tasks.

If hospitals are to survive in a changing health-care system, the philosophy and mandate of hospitals are likely to change. Many hospitals (such as the Caritas Health Group in Edmonton, now a part of the Capital Health Authority) are starting at the beginning and redeveloping their missions and strategic plans with the assistance of community members (O'Connell, 1991). Issues hospitals face include: increasing use of technology, specialization, roles of health-care providers, and utilization of services. These issues are discussed in the following paragraphs.

Increasing Use of Technology

The active-treatment hospital is based on a system consisting of high technology, many procedures, and high costs. Professional literature suggests that about

20,000 new medical devices are invented world-wide each year. Intravenous infusion pumps, electronic thermometers, and other equipment are common on every nursing unit. Dialysis equipment and ventilators can be found in some general nursing areas under certain circumstances.

Computerization offers the potential of saving considerable staff time, but the full effect is yet to be realized. Most hospitals have acquired hospital information systems, and computer terminals are common on every unit (and sometimes at the bedside). These information systems are used to maintain financial, management, and clinical information.

Although the public often views the increasing use of technology negatively, in some instances, such as the use of lithotripsy for renal calculi, angioplasties that reduce the need for coronary artery bypass surgery, and laparoscopic cholecystectomy, the availability of technology markedly reduces the number of days of hospitalization.

In contrast, 40% of hospital administrators have reported that some medical technology is not cost-effective (Kirby, 1992). Although the nursing care of acutely ill patients involves a great deal of technology, the "high tech" must be balanced with "high touch" to provide nursing care of high quality.

Specialization

Specialization is now the norm in the acute-care sector. In university teaching hospitals, units often are organized according to medical subspecialties. Nurses also have become increasingly skilled in particular areas. In nursing, the term specialization is used to include both advanced nursing practice (such as with the clinical nurse specialist) and speciality practice by nurses with basic preparation. The main reason for specialization in clinical practice was the need for competence and effectiveness in the delivery of nursing services.

There are more than 120 specialty organizations and groups in Canada. In 1986, the Canadian Nurses Association established guidelines for designation of specialty nursing associations. A number of specialty nursing organizations (including the Canadian Council for Occupational Health Nursing, the Canadian Association of Nephrology Nurses and Technicians, and the Canadian Neurosciences Nurses Association) are cooperating with the CNA to develop certification examinations.

Although many assume that specialization leads to better care and more efficient use of medical equipment (Kirby, 1992), some are concerned that specialization will result in fragmentation of care. For instance, when a person is hospitalized on a surgical unit, care of comorbid medical conditions is not always optimal. Although the efficiencies of specialization have advantages, care must be taken to ensure holistic care of clients.

Roles of Various Health-Care Providers

A wide variety of health-care providers now work in acute-care facilities. Nurses and professional nursing associations have attempted to define the scope of professional nursing practice, particularly in relation to the role of physicians and the transfer of medical functions, but nursing's relationship to other categories of health-care providers also must be considered. Nurses function both independently and collaboratively with other health professionals. The care that nurses provide in the midst of pain, fear, suffering, loss, birth, death, aging, and grieving has been described as the "privileged place of nursing" (Benner and Wrubel, 1989).

Because the various provinces have different nurse practice and health discipline laws, roles of other health-care workers vary from province to province. In Alberta, for instance, the scope of the licensed practical nurse includes medication administration, physical assessment, specific nursing treatments, health promotion, and psychosocial support. Difficulties arise from the indistinct terms used to describe roles. For instance, physical assessment and health promotion can cover a range of activities, the limits of which are not clear.

In addition, several hospitals are exploring the use of unlicensed staff, who learn about nursing care from working with nurses. However, "the registered nurse is legally accountable for assessing the capabilities of licensed and unlicensed nursing personnel to assure that only those individuals who are truly qualified are delegated responsibility for carrying out specific aspects of nursing care" (Kennerly, 1989). In the current environment of scarce resources and increasing patient acuity, nurses may be unable to find the time to assume this responsibility. Professional associations and unions are concerned about this trend, and the outcomes for patient care are yet to be determined.

The boundaries of nursing in relation to other health care professions will not be easily clarified. We will continue to face changes in educational systems, technology, information systems, hospital organizational patterns, community needs, and economic conditions. However, there should be some agreement about the scopes of practice based on the needs of clients in the health-care system, rather than on the convenience of health-care professionals and bureaucrats.

Utilization of Services

Overall, the number of patients admitted to hospitals in Canada for all diseases has remained fairly constant over the last several decades, at about 16,000 admissions per year per 100,000 population. In 1991, there were 1241 public hospitals in Canada with a total of 169,890 beds (Statistics Canada, 1992). The average patient stay in short-term units/facilities during this time was 8.43 days per patient (Statistics Canada, 1992). With the growth of new technology, procedures such as transplantation, and an aging population, the utilization of hospital beds has become a major issue. Waiting lists for many surgical procedures are extremely long; for some surgical procedures, waiting lists are still up to a year long.

Utilization of Intensive Care Units. The increased utilization of intensive care units (ICU) and the costs incurred as a result of this care are a source of concern. Relatively little data is available on the use of intensive care units in Canada. Between 1969 and 1986, ICU utilization grew by an average rate of 4.8% annually. In 1986, there were 42 ICU days per 1000 population (Jacobs and Noseworthy, 1990). National costs for 1986 were estimated to be $1.03 billion, which is approximately 8% of the total inpatient costs and .2% of Canada's Gross Domestic Product. Although these costs are high, Jacobs and Noseworthy (1990) noted that ICU utilization is 2.5 times higher in the United States. They also addressed the importance of obtaining more information on outcomes and effectiveness of ICU in relation to utilization and costs.

Increased awareness of the costs of critical care has led to many questions about allocation of resources. Many of these questions have major ethical implications. Should oncology patients be treated in intensive care units? Should patients who have a "do not resuscitate" (no-code) order remain in an ICU? These issues are discussed later in this chapter.

Unlike other critical-care units, burn units have had a decrease in admissions in recent years. The admissions dropped from 57 per 100,000 in 1966 to 23 per 100,000 in 1989. The admission rate is three times greater for children under 4 years of age, but this segment has decreased in parallel with the total. Reasons for this change are not entirely clear but seem to be related to economic conditions, fewer industrial accidents, mandatory smoke detectors, and better public education in the prevention of burn injuries (particularly scalds in children) (Snelling and Germann, 1992). This may be an indication that health-promotion activities and a focus on prevention are successful.

Ambulatory Care. The emergency department of the hospital traditionally was viewed as the ambulatory care department. People who require medical and nursing care, whether emergent, acute, or subacute, visit emergency departments, during both daytime and nighttime hours. This pattern has been encouraged to some extent by physicians who often find it more convenient to see the client in the hospital than in the office or home. An average of 73.92 people per day visited each emergency department in Canada in 1991-1992 (Statistics Canada, 1992). This number is higher in teaching hospitals, with an average of 137.79 visits daily, and in pediatric hospitals, at 137.60 visits daily (Statistics Canada, 1992). Although one might expect that the mean number of visits to emergency departments would be decreasing as a result of the growing number of ambulatory care facilities/departments, this does not seem to be the case. The utilization of emergency departments has increased slowly but steadily over time.

A wide variety of diagnostic services and treatments are provided in ambulatory-care departments. These range from blood tests and x-rays to surgical procedures such as laparoscopic cholecystectomies and herniorrhaphies. In 1991-1992, the average number of ambulatory care visits per hospital per day was 147. However, the figures are much higher for teaching and pediatric hospitals; teaching hospitals reported an average of 601.43 visits daily, and pediatric hospitals reported an average of 506.63 visits per day. These also represent an increase over the previous years (Statistics Canada, 1992).

The nature of nursing practice in ambulatory care units also is changing. Until recently, nurses in ambulatory care departments spent much of their time performing clerical duties and assisting physicians. In addition, the nurses did some patient teaching, providing information about illness and treatment. However, a more autonomous professional nursing practice was needed (Feeley and Gerez-Lirette, 1992). Through reallocation of tasks and the use of a professional practice model, nurses in one setting had a significant effect on client outcomes; professional growth of nurses and a positive effect on nursing education also were noted (Feeley and Gerez-Lirette, 1992).

Many hospitals have established preadmission clinics to improve utilization of hospital beds, resulting in savings. Clients visit preadmission clinics in the week or two before surgery. They are assessed by nurses and anesthetists; have diagnostic blood tests, ECGs, x-rays, or other necessary tests; and receive instruction. In some hospitals, preadmission clinics are combined with programs to admit patients on the day of surgery (rather than the day before surgery). These programs have resulted in better utilization of beds, shorter hospitalizations, and high patient satisfaction (LeNoble, 1993).

Partly as a result of the health-care reform movement, the number of services available to the community has grown. In British Columbia and Alberta, regional ambulatory care programs have been established for transplant recipients (Brown, 1990). More self-care dialysis facilities are being established away from the major treatment centres.

Walk-in medical clinics have been established in many cities. These facilities offer people an alternative to use of the emergency and ambulatory care departments at hospitals. These facilities are open for longer hours (often 18 to 24 hours per day) 7 days per week. Nursing care includes assessment, collecting of specimens, teaching, and follow-up (Darcovich, 1987). Medical care covers a range of noncritical care. When necessary, clients are given interim care and transferred to hospital by ambulance.

In British Columbia, a nursing centre is being established by the Ministry of Health through a grant to the Registered Nurses Association of British Columbia. This clinic will provide nurses in this setting with the opportunity to use their skills fully to offer primary health care. In Alberta, nurses have organized nursing clinics to increase the public's awareness of the services directly provided by registered nurses. In Quebec, McGill University School of Nursing has used a professional practice model for some time to provide primary health-care services in ambulatory care settings. (Feeley and Gerez-Lirette, 1992). In the future, we undoubtedly will see nurses providing more acute-care as well as health-promotion services, as part of their mandate for primary health care!

Home Care. Home-care programs are offered through local health units, through other community agencies (such as the Victorian Order of Nurses [VON]), and through hospitals. Programs coordinated through hospitals tend to be extensions of hospital-based programs. For instance, many dialysis centres operate home dialysis programs under the auspices and funding of the hospitals. At the Vancouver General Hospital, individuals awaiting cardiac transplantation return home receiving a continuous intravenous infusion of dobutamine, a positive inotropic agent that increases myocardial contractility (Phillips, 1992). Palliative-care programs have enabled people near death to remain at home, in some cases with access to nursing care on a 24-hour basis (Symons, 1992). Nursing care for these programs often is provided through the hospital, often in conjunction with other community health-care agencies.

Hospital nurses in many cases are actively involved in the development of discharge plans for individuals who normally would be kept in hospital. Kohm (1993) describes the case of a woman on a ventilator who was taught to care for her tracheostomy and manage the technology associated with the ventilator. After 3 1/2 years of hospitalization and a year of discharge planning, the woman was able to live independently with attendant support. The difference in cost between institutionalization and independent living for this one woman was approximately $20,000 per month.

However, managing care at home has many disincentives compared to care in an acute-care hospital. Groft (1992) describes a heartbreaking case of a woman with metastatic breast cancer who absorbed the cost of narcotics and special beds to enable her to die in her home. Although the specific problems were addressed in this geographical area through a proposal that demonstrated the potential cost savings, this set of circumstances continues in other parts of the country.

Mental Health. In Canada, inpatient treatment is one of the main forms of therapy available to people with mental-health problems. Statistics show that about 61% of individuals discharged from psychiatric facilities are women (Miedema and

Stoppard, 1993). There has been a recognition that peoples' experiences with institutionalization for mental illnesses are not always positive. One study of Canadian women who were admitted to psychiatric units found that most of the women felt unnecessarily controlled. However, in retrospect, most agreed that they benefitted from hospitalization; most felt safe and protected in the hospital environment, and some were anxious about leaving the unit (Miedema and Stoppard, 1993).

Various approaches have been used to address the quality-of-life issues associated with psychiatric hospitalization. Leahy, Stout, and Myrah (1991) described the use of a family systems model to provide care to clients in an inpatient mental health unit. The nurses reported very successful outcomes with use of the model, and families reported that they felt more involved in and informed about patient care.

Many psychiatric hospitals have closed; because of this, acute-care city hospitals needed to develop policies and procedures for treatment of formal or certified patients (Shields, 1989). The terms "formal" or "certified" refer to individuals who have been admitted to the hospital under the criteria of the mental health legislation and are unable to leave voluntarily. The length of hospitalization of people formally admitted to acute-care hospitals has tended to be markedly lower than for psychiatric hospitals; in one hospital, the average length of stay for formal patients under a certificate was 15.95 days (Shields, 1989).

Over the last 20 years, people who have various psychiatric disorders increasingly have been deinstitutionalized. Like other clinical areas and medical specialties, psychiatric services are offered on an outpatient basis. Lebrun, Leladhar-Singh, and Luke (1991) described an outpatient education program for schizophrenic adults. Their goals were to help the clients understand their illness, increase their knowledge of medication use, teach them coping skills for illness management, and increase their ability to use support systems in the community. Although the authors have not formally evaluated the program, they reported that they had very positive results.

Community mental-health nurses link with hospitals, communities, and government to provide an integrated network of mental-health services. They are involved in community education, direct client services, consultation, program development, and research (Power, 1991). In the area of prevention of mental illness, the community mental-health nurse might provide information on topics such as parenting or stress management; in the area of secondary prevention aimed at reducing the severity and duration of illness, the nurse may help provide crisis intervention; and in the area of tertiary prevention, the community mental-health nurse may assist in case management of clients with chronic mental illness (Power, 1991).

As in other areas of the health-care sector, consumers of mental-health services and their families increasingly are involved and empowered. In 1987, the Canadian Mental Health Association developed an initiative to increase consumer involvement in service planning and decision-making. The association obtained federal funding to establish boards that represented consumers, family, informal helpers, formal services (i.e., hospitals and community mental-health services), and community agencies (Pyke, Samuelson, Shepherd, and Brown, 1991). As a result, new structures were established to encourage greater consumer involvement. Mental-health agencies and psychiatric units are establishing councils and committees to increase clients' control of issues in the delivery of services.

Care of Children. Many acute-care hospitals have one or more pediatric units for the care of acutely ill children. Larger cities also tend to have pediatric hospitals. No pediatric facilities are available in smaller centres, however, and children either must be transported to a larger centre or receive care in hospital units with adults.

Some major teaching hospitals have developed transport teams to facilitate the rapid and safe transport of premature infants and acutely ill children to a major tertiary-care hospital. Nurses working on these transport teams have highly specialized skills and expanded roles that permit them to intervene early in the event of life-threatening emergencies.

Like other areas of the acute-care sector, ambulatory care facilities for children have grown markedly. Some general hospitals have developed separate emergency- and ambulatory-care departments for children, recognizing the unique needs of children.

In addition to outpatient clinics and day-surgery facilities, some hospitals have developed care-by-parent units. Parents assume responsibility for the provision of care; normally a nurse works during the day to teach parents to provide this care for their child during the acute illnesses. During the evening and night, nursing assistance is available on request from an adjacent nursing unit.

In recent years, many hospital-based and community programs have been developed to prevent injury. Because accidents are the primary cause of morbidity and mortality in Canadian children, such programs can have a major effect on the acute-care sector. Nurses and other professionals have established programs on topics such as the use of car seats, safety on playgrounds, use of bicycle helmets, poison control, trampoline safety, and dangers of cords on blinds.

Maternity Care. Childbirth might seem to be an inappropriate topic in the context of acute care, because childbirth is a normal physiological event. However, in Canada at this time, nearly all women deliver their babies in a hospital. This has resulted in the use of considerable technology and many medical interventions. Many hospitals now use birthing rooms, which have a more natural, homelike environment. Nevertheless, the norm is still an OR-like case room with nurses in surgical garb.

In Canada, the average length of postpartum stays has decreased to about 3.9 days (Rush and Valaitis, 1992). Many hospitals have planned and implemented early postpartum discharge programs, in which low-risk women and babies are discharged within 48 hours of an uncomplicated delivery (Fortier-Bates, 1993). These programs have been found to be safe and cost-effective. However, consumers still need home supports. In one study these included a 24-hour hotline, free supplies, daily nursing visits for 1 week, and homemaker assistance (Rush and Valaitis, 1992).

Alberta and Ontario recently passed laws that permit the practice of midwifery. A midwife provides independent health care for both mother and baby throughout pregnancy, labour, birth, and the postpartum period. Some have argued that midwifery should be recognized as a profession separate from nursing. Many midwives believe that the current practices and cultures of nursing practice may be difficult to change and that the chance of success would be greater if a new discipline were established. "Midwives who are nurses would be too accepting of the hierarchical way in which hospitals are run ... would not have the flexibility of independent professionals" (Eberts, 1987). A baccalaureate program in midwifery was initiated jointly in the fall of 1993 by McMaster University, Laurentian University, and the Ryerson Polytechnical Institute. The University of Alberta also offers a midwifery minor in the Master of Nursing program. Midwifery practice probably will grow in Canada as other provinces develop legislation that permits midwives to practise.

Although home births have been found to be safe in low-risk pregnancies (Edmonton Midwifery Group, 1988; Tyson, 1991), members of the medical profession still actively discourage home births. Nevertheless, some couples choose this option. An increasing number of expectant parents privately pay for midwives for prenatal and childbirth care (Hanley, 1993) because health-care insurance plans do not currently fund midwives. However, the Ontario Minister of Health was quoted as saying that her next priority is to obtain reimbursement for midwifery through the provincial health insurance plan (Midwifery, 1993). Standards of practice for midwives are being developed, and midwives probably will become much more prominent health care professionals.

Chronic Health Challenges in the Acute-Care Sector. In Canada, approximately 11% of the population is over 65 years of age. By 1999, 13% of the population is predicted to be over 65. The proportion of the population in the hospital ranges from less than 1% of those age 65 to 69 to 5.1% of those age 90 years or more. Kirby projected that by the end of the 1990s, 51% of hospital patient days will be used by people over 65 (1992). Because of this trend, Abernathy and Lentjes projected that in Calgary alone, a city of 600,000 people, an additional 600 beds would be required by the year 2000 (1990). Abernathy and Lentjes also noted that elderly occupied almost 30% of the total number of eligible acute-care (not including pediatric and obstetric) beds in the city's hospitals. If those elderly individuals awaiting placement in a long-term-care facility were excluded, this figure would be reduced to 23%.

One problem is that a significant number of acute-care hospital beds are being occupied by people requiring long-term care. However, for many elderly people, an acute-care hospital is the point of entry into the long-term-care system. Patients awaiting long-term care often have been called "bed blockers," and health-care professionals have not addressed their specific rehabilitative and palliative needs.

In an attempt to provide better care to long-term-care patients, many hospitals have established special units for care of chronically ill older adults (Carson and Ross, 1993). The goal of these units is to "cultivate a therapeutic social environment that would be more home-like and less structured, thus enhancing the quality of life of residents" (Carson and Ross, 1993). At Queensway-Carleton Hospital in Nepean, Ontario, a community-development approach was used to identify the values and activities residents and staff viewed as important. Residents wanted to be as active, informed, and involved as possible (Carson and Ross, 1993). The hospital changed the environment to improve their quality of life, including adding reading materials with large print, greater time with all care providers, call bells in all areas, including lounges, a place where children could visit, and an area with the atmosphere of a dining room.

Many special-care units have been established for individuals with dementias such as Alzheimer's disease. Because resources are limited, admission to these units has been limited (Wilden and Froese, 1991).

With a growing elderly population, the use of acute-care beds probably will increase. However, hospitals are not well suited to meeting the present and future needs of the elderly. We need concerted effort to provide more holistic care and to give the elderly opportunities for greater decision-making and self-determination. We also need more community-based services for the elderly, such as day care, group homes, and transportation.

Adult day programs are offered in many different settings. Some are physically located in a hospital or a long-term-care facility. Others are located in offices in the community. Many different services are offered in day programs. Some programs have a social/recreational focus and offer family caregivers the opportunity for respite. Other programs have more nursing involvement and may provide services such as bathing, footcare, and case management. Some programs are specifically designed for cognitively impaired elderly.

Adult day programs generally are distinguished from day hospitals, and government funding has been tied to the classification. Generally, day programs are designed for long-term care, and day hospitals are intended more for acute-care and short-term care. Many day hospitals offer diagnostic tests, treatments, and regular medical care. Some actively focus on assessment and rehabilitation. However, these distinctions are not clear, with some day hospitals offering services similar to day programs. Nevertheless, adult day programs offer much-needed acute care as well as chronic care.

In the Victoria Health Project, it was demonstrated that hospitals can work in partnership with large and small community agencies to coordinate care for the elderly. A $4 million initiative began in 1988 to prevent hospitalization of the elderly and support family caregivers. This program included a "quick response team," with nurses on call to respond to emergencies of senior citizens. The outcome was a substantial reduction in admissions to acute-care hospitals. The coordination and delivery of appropriate health services was the ultimate goal; the communication and discussion between agencies was also identified as a positive outcome.

■ Acute Care in the Canadian North

Acute care of adults and children in Canada's north is very different from that in the rest of the country because of the low population density. Because the population in the north is so sparse, hospitals do not form the centre of the health-care system. Much of the health care in rural areas of the north is provided in nursing stations or health centres, where one or more nurses provide individually based acute care and community health care. The scope of practice of these nurses is very broad and includes emergency care such as suturing, medical functions such as prescribing medications, and preventive health activities such as immunization and teaching. Physicians periodically visit clinics. In emergency situations, patients are moved to hospitals in major centres, in either Yellowknife or Whitehorse, or to the southern hospitals.

Most pregnant women now are encouraged to go south for hospital deliveries several weeks before their estimated date of confinement (Herbert, 1989). This move has substantially reduced infant and maternal mortality; the infant mortality rate for Inuit babies went from 95 to 38 per 1000 live births between 1971 and 1981 (Report on Health Conditions in the Northwest Territories, 1982).

Although Canada overall has a very low infant and maternal mortality rate, fetal and neonatal mortality rates are 40% higher in natives than nonnatives (Thomson, 1990). This has been attributed to poor socioeconomic conditions. In both Ontario and British Columbia, heavy birthweights were 50% more common in native than nonnative groups. Observers hypothesized that natives have unusually high rates of glucose intolerance during pregnancy.

Technology and medical care are limited in the small isolated communities of Canada's north. Cultural differences also must be considered; in the Northwest Territories, for example, the population consists of approximately 35% Inuit, 20%

native Indian, and 45% other Canadians (usually from the south). In 1960, in an attempt to meet the health-care needs of aboriginal people, the federal government (through the Medical Services Branch [MSB]) developed a category of health-care workers called community health representatives (CHRs). CHRs are trained by MSB through a series of short courses ranging from several weeks to several months in length. The CHR's role is to bridge the cultural gaps in health care, increase cross-cultural communication, and focus on prevention of illness. They are encouraged to empower people to deal with their problems, including drug- and alcohol-related problems (Manuel, 1992).

The successes of the CHR programs have not been well documented. Some aboriginal people have been concerned that the CHR programs have not been effective. They believe that many of them spend much of their time trying to arrange illness care, particularly for sick children and elders, and that CHRs should receive more formal education and recognition, given the complexity of their work.

■ Ethical Issues in Acute Care

When Canadian nurses talk of the major issues they face in the care of acutely ill people, they inevitably identify ethical issues. Questions about allocation of resources and prolongation of life inevitably arise. These issues are not easily resolved and often differ from the issues in the United States and other countries. MacPhail and Ross Kerr address some of the unique perspectives for Canadian nurses in Chapter 2. In the following paragraphs, the main ethical issues relating to acute care are highlighted.

Allocation of Resources

Because the costs of health care have been such an issue, the allocation of scarce resources also has become an issue. Treatments such as dialysis therapy, cancer therapy, treatment of AIDS, transplantation, neonatal intensive care, and open heart surgery have come under increasing scrutiny. For example, over a 7-year period from 1979 to 1985, the province of Ontario reported a 52% increase in coronary artery bypass surgery. In 1992, the cost of bypass surgery was $40,000. However, although bypass surgery appears to relieve pain in 75% to 85% of patients, this relief lasts only a limited time. Bypass surgery does not appear to extend life or prevent myocardial infarction (Cortese, 1992). Similarly, questions have been raised about many of the outcomes associated with the use of other treatments and procedures in acute care (Rachlis and Kushner, 1989).

Prolongation of Life

Questions about prolongation of life arise frequently in nursing practice. Nurses wonder: Why is a 95-year-old man receiving dialysis? Why do we try to save very small premature infants in neonatal intensive care units? Do we resuscitate patients who have indicated that they do not wish to be resuscitated? Should a person who is not to receive CPR be maintained in an ICU? Nurses know that quality of life does not always come with quantity of life.

Many of these questions regarding prolongation of life could be resolved through the use of advance directives or living wills. Advance treatment directives give individuals the opportunity to make their own decisions about the use of extraordinary measures in preserving life (Anderson, Gludue, Laurie, Skotniski, and Tramer, 1991). In Alberta, legislation recently was proposed for use of advance directives and designation of a proxy or decision-maker for people who are unable to make decisions for themselves.

However, the use of advance directives is not widespread in Canada. In their Canadian study, Singer and Hughes (1991) found that 85% of Canadian family physicians support the use of advance directives. However, 80% of the respondents reported that they had never cared for an incompetent patient with an advance treatment directive.

Physicians, nurses, and patients differ in their attitudes toward advance directives. In one study, Perry, Nicholas, Molzahn, and Dossetor (1993) found that 79% of patients with end stage renal disease wanted to discuss advance directives. However, 52% of this sample agreed that major treatment decisions should be left to the physician. Physicians believed that treatment options including advance directives should be discussed with patients and their families but should not be put in written form. Most nurses (86%) believed that advance directives should be discussed with patients and that directives should be written. These differences suggest that individuals and health-care professionals need to discuss this issue much more thoroughly so that the wishes of the affected individual can be respected.

Many hospitals have faced the issues of prolongation of life. One study (Singer, cited in Wilson, 1993), reported that 51% of Canadian acute-care hospitals had policies regarding life support, including "do not resuscitate" (DNR) policies. However, provinces varied considerably; in one province, 17% of acute-care hospitals had policies about end-of-life life support; at the other end of the range, in another province, 79% of the acute-care hospitals had these policies. In contrast, DNR policies are required by the Joint Accreditation Commission for every accredited acute-care hospital in the United States (Edwards, 1990).

Euthanasia and assisted suicide are not legal in Canada. However, cases such as that of Sue Rodriguez, a young mother with Lou Gehrig's disease who sought the right to assisted suicide, have drawn public attention and sympathy. A Supreme Court judgment upheld the status quo and did not recommend the legalization of assisted suicide. Interestingly, Sue Rodriguez did commit suicide and was assisted by a physician whose identification remained secret. The event occurred in the presence of a sympathetic member of Parliament from British Columbia. Thus the controversy continues.

Ethics of Caring

Because of the increasing concern over ethical issues, the literature is growing and more courses are being offered on ethics in health care. The goals of many ethics courses and programs for nurses have included sensitization to and identification of ethical issues, application of ethical reasoning in resolving questions arising from controversial issues, and the use of the ethical principles that should be considered (i.e., autonomy, beneficence, nonmaleficence, and distributive justice). In many cases, however, two or more principles must be considered and may in fact conflict with each other. Schattschneider suggested that principle-based or theory-based ethics do not help the clinician make ethical decisions (1992). The answer seems to lie in an ethic of caring. A holistic caring perspective that considers the cultural contexts and differences in values and health-care practices may help health-care professionals consider all possible consequences and come to the best possible decisions.

◼ The Future of Acute Care

The acute-care sector has changed rapidly as a result of many factors. Spiraling health-care costs, the increasing emphasis on humanism in health care, and the increase in self-care programs have changed the characteristics of acute care dramatically. Although hospitals once were the centres of health care, the future is likely to bring hospitals without walls and hospitals without beds. A variety of programs have been developed to meet the needs of special groups such as children, women, the elderly, aboriginal people, and immigrants. Many of these programs are based on ambulatory-care or home-care facilities. In the future, we will need to continue to develop policies and programs that consider the specific needs of various groups and the cultures of our communities.

Unfortunately, we have conducted relatively little research to evaluate the outcomes of our approaches. This research becomes increasingly important as we struggle to demonstrate the cost effectiveness of nursing care in an environment of economic constraint.

Nursing in acute-care settings promises to become even more complex. Nurses will need a broad educational background to address the issues that they will face. We cannot easily prepare practitioners who can function as easily in an intensive care unit as in a community agency. Only through the innovation and creativity of nurses will the health-care system be able to meet the challenges of the future.

■ REFERENCES

Abernathy, T.J., & Lentjes, D.M. (1990). A three-year census of dependent elderly. *Canadian Journal of Public Health, 81*, 22-26.

Anderson, J.M. (1990). Home care management in chronic illness and the self-care movement: An analysis of ideologies and economic processes influencing policy decision. *Advances in Nursing Science, 12*(2), 71-83.

Anderson, M., Gludue, S., Laurie, M., Skotniski, E., & Tramer, D. (1991). The living will issue: Who has the right to choose? *Canadian Nurse, 87*(11), 37-39.

Benner, P., & Wrubel, J. (1989). *The primacy of caring.* Don Mills, ON: Addison Wesley.

Brown, L. (1990). Transplant program expands: Six regional ambulatory clinics planned. *RNABC News, 22*(2), 13-14.

Carson, M.M., & Ross, M.M. (1993). Changing the model of practice: Geriatric long term care in an acute care hospital. *Canadian Nurse, 89*(2), 35-38.

Cortese, F. (1992). Chelation therapy: The bypass alternative? *Canadian Nurse, 88*(11), 11-12.

Darcovich, O. (1987). Walk-in clinics: New opportunities for nurses. *RNABC News, 19*(3), 22-23.

Edmonton Midwifery Group. (1988). *Statistics: Edmonton homebirths 1980-1988.* Edmonton: Edmonton Midwifery Group.

Eberts, M. (1987). *Report of the task force on the implementation of midwifery in Ontario.* Toronto: Ontario Ministry of Health.

Edwards, B.S. (1990). Does the DNR patient belong in the ICU? *Critical Care Nursing Clinics of North America, 2*(3), 473-480.

Fortier-Bates, L. (1993). Edmonton's short stay maternity programs. *AARN Newsletter, 49*(4), 18-19.

Feeley, N., & Gerez-Lirette, T. (1992). Development of professional practice based on the McGill model of nursing in an ambulatory care setting. *Journal of Advanced Nursing, 17*, 801-808.

Groft, J. (1992). At home with pain. *Canadian Nurse, 88*(8), 36-37.

Growe, S.J. (1991). *Who cares: The crisis in Canadian nursing.* Toronto: McLelland and Stewart.

Hanley, F. (1993). Midwife-friendly care. *Canadian Nurse, 89*(2), 13-16.

Herbert, P. (1989). A midwife in the Canadian arctic? *Midwife Health Visitor and Community Nurse, 25*, 414-418.

Irvine, D., & Dreger, L. (1991). Women as informal caregivers. *Canadian Nurse, 87*, 22-23.

Jacobs, P., & Noseworthy, T.W. (1990). National estimates of intensive care utilization and costs: Canada and the United States. *Critical Care Medicine, 18*, 1282-1286.

Johnson, M.W., Coombs, G.W., & Wood, V.M. (1991). Merger and medical staff: An approach to integration. *Health Care Management Forum, 4*(2), 32-38.

Kennerly, S.M. (1989). Implications of the use of unlicensed personnel: A nursing perspective. *Focus on Critical Care, 16*(5), 364-368?

Kirby, M. (1992). The economics and politics of health care system ailments. *AARN Newsletter, 48*(6), 10-13.

Leahy, M., Stout, L., & Myrah, I. (1991). Family systems nursing. *Canadian Nurse, 87*(2), 31-33.

Lebrun, L.J., Leladhar-Singh, M., & Luke, A. (1991). Schizophrenic outpatient education. *Canadian Nurse, 87*(5), 25-27.

LeNoble, E. (1993). Preadmission clinics: Gaining ground. *Nursing BC, 25*(4), 21-24.

Manuel, R. (1992). The story of the CHR. *Healthsharing, 13*(1), 31-37.

Miedema, J.M., & Stoppard, J.M. (1993). Understanding women's experiences of psychiatric hospitalization. *Canada's Mental Health, 41*(1), 2-6.

Monk, M.C., & Edgar, L. (1991). Restructuring to create a climate for clinical excellence in nursing. *Health Care Management Forum, 4*(2), 22-27.

Nanowski, A. (1992). Nursing in a northern isolated post. *AARN Newsletter, 48*(7), 7-8.

New directions: The changing face of health care in British Columbia. (1993). *Victoria: Ministry of Health.*

O'Brien-Pallas, L. (1992). Overview of nursing research in health care within the current economic context. *Canadian Journal of Nursing Administration, 5*(2), 20-24.

O'Connell, P. (1991). Role statement: One hospital's experience. *Health Care Management Forum, 4*(2), 28-31.

Perry, F., & Code, S. (1991). Shared governance: A Canadian experience. *Canadian Journal of Nursing Administration, 4*(2), 27-30.

Perry, L.D., Nicholas, D., Molzahn, A.E., & Dossetor, J.B. (1993). Attitudes of dialysis patients and care givers regarding advance directives and decision-making. Unpublished paper, University of Alberta Hospitals.

Phillips, P. (1992). Home dobutamine. *Canadian Nurse, 88*, 13-15.

Power, J. (1991). The expanding role of community mental health nurses. *Canadian Nurse, 87*(5), 20-21.

Pyke, J., Samuelson, G.P., Shepherd, & Brown, N. (1991). Shaping mental health services. *Canadian Nurse, 87*(5), 17-19.

Rachlis, M., & Kushner, C. (1989). *Second opinion: What's wrong with Canada's health care system and how to fix it.* Toronto: Collins.

Registered Nurses Association of British Columbia. (1990). *Health promotion: A discussion paper.* Vancouver: the Association.

Registered Nurses Association of British Columbia. (1992). *Determinants of health: Empowering strategies for nursing practice: A background paper.* Vancouver: the Association.

Report on Health Conditions in the North West Territories (1982). Yellowknife: Northwest Territories Government.

Rush, J.P., & Valaitis, R.K. (1992). Postpartum care: Home or hospital? *Canadian Nurse, 88*(5), 29-31.

Schattschneider, H. (1992). Ethics for the nineties: Will nurses continue to care? *Canadian Nurse, 88*(11), 16-18.

Seaton, P.D., Evans, R.G., Ford, M.G., Fyke, K.J., Sinclair, D.R., & Webber, W.A. (1991). *Closer to home: Summary of the report of the British Columbia royal commission on health care and costs.* Victoria: Crown Publications.

Shields, G. (1989). The treatment of formal patients in a city hospital. *AARN Newsletter, 45*(4), 27-28.

Singer, P.A., & Hughes, D.L. (1991). Family physicians' attitudes towards advance directives. *Clinical Research, 39*(2), abstract 416.

Snelling, C.F.T., & Germann, E.T. (1992). Trends in hospital care of burns in Canada. *Journal of Trauma, 33*, 264-265.

Statistics Canada. (1992). *Health Reports* (catalogue number 82-003S4), 3(2). Ottawa: Minister of Supply and Services Canada.

Symons, D.M. (1992). Palliative response team. *Canadian Nurse, 88*, 36-37.

Thomson, M. (1990). Heavy birthweight in Native Indians of British Columbia. *Canadian Journal of Public Health, 81*, 443-446.

Tyson, H. (1991). Outcomes of 1001 midwife-attended homebirths in Toronto 1983-1988. *Birth, 18*(1), 14-19.

Wilden, B.M., & Froese, K. (1991). Admission criteria for a special care unit for residents with dementia. *Canadian Journal of Nursing Administration, 4*(3), 17-21.

Wilson, D.M. (1993). The influences for do-not-resuscitate policies and end-of-life treatment or non-treatment decisions. Unpublished doctoral dissertation, University of Alberta, Edmonton.

5 PRIMARY HEALTH CARE AND THE HEALTH OF FAMILIES

LINDA REUTTER AND MARGARET J. HARRISON

Primary health care (PHC) is identified by the World Health Organization as the means for achieving an acceptable standard of health for people worldwide using current resources. After discussing inequities in health care at the Thirtieth World Health Assembly in 1977, the World Health Organization met at Alma Ata in an international conference on PHC. The Alma Ata conference published the following definition of PHC: "Essential health care made universally accessible to individuals and families, through their full participation, and at a cost the community and the country can afford" (WHO, 1978). The principles of PHC as the basis of health planning were reaffirmed by the World Health Organization at Riga in 1988 (WHO, 1988).

With increasing concern about the cost of the current Canadian health-care system, governments, health professionals, health economists, and the public have discussed reforming the health-care system. The Canadian Nurses Association (CNA) has declared support for PHC as the means to achieve "Health for All." To outline its position, the CNA has prepared several documents (CNA, 1988; CNA, 1989) in which it proposes that nurses be active participants in a health-care system organized on PHC principles.

The five principles of PHC are: accessibility of services, increased emphasis on prevention and promotion, lay participation, intersectoral cooperation, and appropriate technology. The principle of accessibility means essential care is accessible to the whole community in a manner that is acceptable to the community. Under this principle, health care services would be planned to address inequities in health care experienced by community groups. PHC focuses on health rather than illness. This goal is achieved by placing an emphasis on promotive and preventive care rather than curative care in the planning and provision of health services. In the principle of lay participation, consumers become active partners with professionals, administrators, and governments in health-care planning, delivery, and evaluation. The principle of intersectoral cooperation recognizes the contribution of nonhealth agencies to the health of a nation. Health is linked closely to the economic, educational, and physical environments in which people live and work. Therefore health care is best achieved when the social and economic sectors of the community work cooperatively with the health-care sector. To provide accessible services equitably to the community, primary health-care principles promote the use of technology that is affordable to the community and available to all.

Although some Canadian nurses have provided PHC in the past, the focus on PHC has increased in recent years. This chapter describes recent trends in Canadian nursing that reflect the principles of PHC. The increasing importance of PHC principles in planning health programs has raised a number of issues for nursing practice. This chapter also discusses issues in nursing education related to the increasing emphasis on PHC.

■ Current Examples of Primary Health Care in Canada

PHC principles are evident in many nursing activities in Canada (see CNA, 1988, 1992 for examples). Some of the PHC activities occur in traditional settings, and other PHC projects are located in innovative and unique settings. Because PHC is an approach to providing not only health-care services but also a concept of health care (WHO, 1978; Krebs, 1983), the principles can be applied to some degree within existing structures and services.

Some Canadian nurses began incorporating the principles of PHC into their practice before the Alma Ata conference. In particular, public health nurses provided care that was community-based and that had a preventive or health-promotion focus. Members of the community were involved in planning and administering these programs. In addition, nurses working in northern and remote areas worked with small communities to provide health-care using minimal resources. Other nurses emphasized the importance of self-care practices and the individual's contribution to his own well-being. The following discussion of the role of nurses in PHC includes examples from traditional health-care settings as well as innovative settings.

Public Health Nursing Services

The work of public health nurses (PHNs) in public health units incorporates the principles of PHC (Jones and Craig, 1988; Mills and Ready, 1988). Public health science addresses human health within the broader context of the life process of the community. PHNs are concerned with providing comprehensive, essential services to the entire community, with an emphasis on health promotion and the prevention of illness and injury, especially in the family. Client self-determination is a key concept in public health nursing.

The social influences on health increasingly are seen as legitimate targets of nursing interventions, as PHNs work collaboratively with other disciplines and non-health sectors to promote healthy public policy. These organizations collaborate through organizations such as the Canadian Public Health Association (CPHA). This interdisciplinary organization, in its Position Paper on Healthy Public Policy (CPHA, 1989), recognized that Canadians varied in their access to food, shelter, work, education, and income. CPHA argues that these inequities could be addressed through changes in public policy (CPHA, 1990). Public health nurses through provincial branches of the Community Health Nurses Association of Canada also increasingly support healthy public policy by presenting to government organizations the roles that they fulfil in the community and the issues that patients and families face.

PHNs work with community groups to identify and meet community needs at the community level. However, they have learned that they need better preparation in community development skills to function effectively in this role (Working Group, 1991).

To make health care "culturally accessible" to aboriginal peoples, PHNs may be assisted by community health representatives. For example, in Whitehorse, Yukon, the local First Nations Community has its own health clinic, staffed by one nurse and community health representatives, who are employed by and accountable to the band. The programs at the clinic are designed to meet the needs of this particular community (CNA, 1992).

Centres with Outreach to Underserved Populations

Two agencies that use a multidisciplinary team to bring health care to the inner city population are the Centretown Community Health Centre in Ottawa and the Boyle-McCauley Health Centre in Edmonton, Alberta. In both centres, physicians hold salaried positions and the centre is governed by a board of community representatives.

During the 1980s, the Centretown Community Health Centre board and staff recognized a shift in the population that they served, with increasing numbers of impoverished individuals living in rooming houses and on the street. The Centre developed an outreach program in which nurses make weekly visits to two community drop-in centres. The nurses provide services such as health assessments, health education, and referrals to other agencies. These nurses also work with other organizations to address issues such as poor housing, illiteracy, and unemployment (personal communication, Jane McDonald, August 1993).

Boyle-McCauley Health Centre (BMHC) is a street-front, walk-in clinic whose main mission is to provide easily accessible health care to an inner-city community. This agency also demonstrates many principles of PHC. It provides both medical care and health care focusing on health promotion and illness and injury prevention. The BMHC employs nurse-practitioners, physicians, dietitians, volunteers, mental health consultants, psychologists, and addiction counselors. Staff members at the BMHC collaborate closely with other inner-city agencies. The services are based on the needs of the community and include programs such as needle exchanges, a foot care clinic, and mental health counseling. In addition to clinic services, three nurses conduct home visits to provide primary care, health assessment, and health educa-tion to seniors, expectant and new mothers, and chronically ill individuals. In a man-ner similar to the Centretown Community Health Centre, staff at BMHC attempt to contact others who need health care through outreach programs in rooming houses and halfway houses. BMHC has just secured funding for a dental clinic and is now offering dental services as well. BMHCs involvement in a community economic development project exemplifies the agency's commitment to the interrelationship between health and social and economic development (BMHC, 1993).

Victorian Order of Nurses

The Victorian Order of Nurses (VON) is a voluntary agency with a primary health-care philosophy and a long history of innovation in meeting the needs of the community. VON provides community services that promote, maintain, and improve health, and enhance independence and quality of life. A recently completed project called PEP (Promoting Elders Participation) involved seniors in rural under-served areas in assessing their needs and establishing services to meet them. Another VON initiative is the VON primary health-care clinic in Lark Harbour, New found-land. This clinic was built by local residents and meets community needs for services such as seniors' health counseling, fitness, weight control, foot-care clinics, and pre-natal education and followup (VON, 1992b). The VON also is part of a new "Quick Response Program" in two Windsor, Ontario hospitals. The VON collaborates with other agencies, such as the hospitals, the home-care program, and visiting home-maker agencies, to help prevent hospital admissions. When seniors arrive in emer-gency departments, they are assessed and if possible sent home, where a team of health-care workers can be sent to prevent institutionalization (VON, 1992a).

Nurses as Access to Health Care

A new health-care program that expands nursing practice in the area of PHC is the McAdam Project in New Brunswick, opened in 1993. This project provides both community health-care programs and emergency services under one roof. Nurses coordinate the service, complete the initial client history, assess and analyze health-care needs, provide care, and refer clients to other professionals as needed. The physician in the project is part of the team and has a salaried position. Others are developing community health services based on a nursing assessment of community needs. Future services may include well-child clinics, developmental screening, and immunization clinics. Nurses also will help provide outreach services and develop links with existing community resources. A multidisciplinary team, including members of the community, will continue to evaluate community needs and develop additional programs with available resources (Penny Short, personal communication, August 1993).

The Registered Nurses Association of Nova Scotia is cosponsoring with the Department of Health and the Sacred Heart Hospital a 3-year primary health-care project in Cheticamp, Nova Scotia. In this project, which commenced in November 1992, the nurse is the primary health-care provider and gives patients direct care in addition to providing health education to health personnel and the public, acting as an advocate for the community, and managing and supervising the primary health-care services (Parent, 1993).

■ Issues in PHC

These Canadian services that incorporate PHC principles suggest that nurses are well-positioned to incorporate PHC principles into their nursing practice. Before nurses can fully participate in health-care delivery, however, there is a need to establish an overall strategy for health in Canada, with clear objectives and goals (RNABC, 1990a). Until a national plan for health care is developed, the following issues continue to prevent the full realization of PHC.

Removing Financial Barriers to Accessible Health Care

In spite of Canada's universal health-care insurance, many essential health services are not publicly insured, thus making accessibility income-dependent. For example, working low-income families may not receive extended health-care benefits from their employees, including dental care, prescription drugs, special medical services, and optometry. Premiums for these services, in addition to the regular health premiums, may be too high for families who are already at or near the poverty line (FSA and ISAC, 1991). Cutbacks in Aids to Living equipment may reduce the self-care and independence of physically disabled individuals in the community (RNABC, 1990a). At a time when "stress" is the major health concern for many Canadians (Health and Welfare Canada, 1993), mental health counseling services by providers other than physicians are not insured to the same extent as services provided by psychiatrists in provinces such as Alberta.

Although the impetus for restructuring the health-care system toward a PHC model comes in part from the rising cost of health care, the current fiscal crisis resulting from an increasingly burdensome public debt may undermine important PHC concepts that currently are protected by the Canada Health Act. For example, the introduction of user fees in Canada, currently being considered to offset rising health-care costs, may create financial barriers to accessible health care, particularly for those on fixed incomes. Privatization of health-care services also may contribute to a "two-tiered" health-care system. The CNA has argued that nurses must become politically active in preserving a Canadian health-care system that is universally accessible, comprehensive, portable, and publicly administered (CNA, August 1993).

Determining Essential Services

Essential health care includes a range of services encompassing promotion, prevention, rehabilitation, and support, in addition to curative services (WHO, 1978). Each of these areas should receive the level of resources that reflects its contribution to the health of the population (CNA, 1988; RNABC, 1990a). When resources are limited, only curative services may be considered essential, with the result that needed rehabilitation and health-promotion services are underfunded. With the introduction of short-stay hospital programs, more acutely ill clients are being discharged into the community. Although short-stay programs are important in providing health care closer to home, adequate community resources must be available to support these individuals. Without increased funding at the community level to accommodate this shift, current resources in the community may be shifted to meet the immediate needs of these clients, to the neglect of health-promotion and illness-prevention services.

Although many federal and provincial government health documents incorporate PHC principles (Epp, 1986; Premier's Commission, 1989), governments often allocate inadequate resources to community-based care, particularly health promotion and disease prevention. In Canada, only 3% to 5% of health expenditures are allocated to health promotion and community health services (CNA, 1988). The RNABC (1990b), in its submission to the Royal Commission on Health Care and Costs, reported that the core programs provided by public health units to support family health, although directed toward primary prevention and health promotion for all families, increasingly are being directed toward only high-risk families because of inadequate funding.

Appropriate Use of Personnel

Socially acceptable and affordable methods of health-care delivery include administrative and organizational structures, where the method of payment of health-care professionals and the appropriate use of personnel are important issues. Nurses have argued that health care in Canada could be made more accessible and affordable through expansion of the nurse's role in providing health services and by giving clients direct access to nursing services (RNABC, 1990a; CNA, 1988, 1993; AARN, 1993). Nurses, as a point of entry to the health-care system, are prepared to perform initial assessments, help clients define needs, work with clients in meeting those needs, and direct clients to the most appropriate care providers. In its emphasis on health-care reform, the CNA is concentrating on the unique role that nurses can play in making quality health care accessible and affordable without compromising the five principles of Canada's Medicare system. This expanded role is rooted in health promotion and illness prevention and therefore is much more than simply assuming some medical functions currently performed by physicians.

Professionals have vested interests in their traditional roles, however, which may hinder nurses in expanding their roles and in making these new nursing services publicly insurable and directly accessible to clients. For example, the practice of midwifery in British Columbia (RNABC, 1990a) and in Alberta until 1992 was blocked by the medical practitioners. Recognition must also be given to the role of nonprofessionals and traditional practitioners in providing entry to the health-care system. Nurses must support the use of community health workers and traditional practitioners to make care more culturally accessible and relevant (Shestowsky, 1992).

The issue of appropriate use of personnel arose in the previously discussed McAdam project. Here the Minister of Health, physicians, and nurses agreed on the expanded scope of nursing practice, with nurses providing direct access to the health-care system. However, such involvement would require changes to the Hospital Services Act. In this situation, professionals are constrained by existing legislation and a reticence to open the Act (Penny Short, personal communication, August 1993).

Broadening the Concept of Health

In addition to providing access to health care, PHC recognizes the link between health and the economic and social dimensions of a community. Health is concerned with overall human development and is viewed as a resource that enables people to live socially and economically productive lives (WHO, 1984). Many major health problems confronting families in Canada today, such as family violence and substance abuse, are embedded in social environments. The adverse effects of poverty on individual, family, and community health are well documented (Blackburn, 1991; Kaplan-Sanoff, et al., 1991; Wilkins, 1988). Political, social, and cultural forces directly affect health by limiting access to conditions conducive to good health as well as through their influence on personal health behaviors. Nurses must recognize that individual choices are influenced by environmental supports and constraints. To make environments more health-enhancing rather than health-inhibiting, nurses may need to use social-action strategies that target social institutions rather than individuals. A socioecological view of health also acknowledges that policies in nonhealth sectors influence community health; therefore intersectoral collaboration is required to ensure that all public policy enhances health.

Nurses traditionally have used individualistic models of health behavior and change to improve individual and family health (Butterfield, 1990). Such approaches use psychological theories to explain patterns of health and health care (Dreher, 1982) and focus on altering client attitudes and knowledge rather than altering the environment or empowering clients to do so (Butterfield, 1990). An "upstream" focus to preventing family health problems requires thinking more broadly about the economic, political, and environmental factors that inhibit health. New approaches and theoretical frameworks that consider the social determinants of health, such as critical social theory, could give direction to nursing interventions at a societal level (Stevens and Hall, 1992; Kleffel, 1991; Kristjanson and Chalmers, 1991).

Developing Collaboration

All of the major documents on PHC discuss the need for collaborative work. This includes collaboration between clients (mutual aid), between clients and practitioners (self-determination), between practitioners (integrated service), between practitioners and communities (community development), and between communities and governments (building healthy public policy) (RNABC, 1990a). The PHC principle that clients are active participants in identifying and meeting their health needs may require a shift in nurses' concept of the nurse-client interaction.

For collaboration to work, health-care practitioners must be willing to trust people and communities to be responsible for their own health, and to "do with" rather than "do to." Becoming a partner in care rather than a provider of care will require consulting, enabling, and facilitating skills. Current nursing frameworks, such as those developed by Orem (1985) and Neuman (1989), will assist in this change when nurses work with individuals, as these frameworks emphasize client autonomy and self-determination. Working collaboratively with families in a partner relationship is emphasized in the community health nursing literature (e.g., Kristjanson and Chalmers, 1991; Pesznecker, Zerwekh, and Horn, 1989).

The need for collaboration between nurses and clients may be greater in informal support networks (Stewart, 1990). A study of the learning needs of a sector of Canadian nurses regarding lay support groups reported that nurses had inadequate knowledge of specific mutual aid groups, of the benefits and characteristics of self-help, and of community-organization and consulting skills (Stewart, 1989).

This collaboration includes nurses' collaboration with members of other health disciplines. This may be difficult to achieve if disciplines, including nursing, attempt to retain their vested interests and proceed from an adversarial position. For PHC to work, health and social service providers must have open lines of referral.

■ Implications for Nursing Education

The movement toward a greater role for nurses in delivering primary health-care has implications for nurse educators (Innes, 1987). An early study by Edwards and Craig (1987) found that PHC knowledge and skills appeared in Canadian nursing curricula minimally and to a lesser extent than expected. Only 31.4% of nurse educators were aware of the Alma Ata declaration, and 19.6% had read the ICN statement on primary health-care; 88% were unaware of the Canadian government's position on PHC. Moreover, responses indicated poor differentiation between the concepts of primary care, primary nursing, and primary health care.

Tenn and Niskala (1994) conducted a recent study to determine the extent to which Canadian university schools of nursing currently include primary health-care concepts in their undergraduate and graduate curricula. Approximately 60% of the schools were described as having a reasonable degree of integration of PHC in their curricula. Most programs include a health promotion focus and stress intersectoral collaboration for the health of individuals, families, and groups. Collaborative partnership roles with communities were less frequently included. Students rarely obtained clinical experience in settings conducive to public participation.

The definition of health and the importance of collaboration in PHC have implications for nursing education and for nursing practice models.

First, the broad definition of health espoused by PHC means that students require a solid foundation in epidemiology (particularly social epidemiology) and environmental health. Chalmers and Kristjanson (1989) suggest that the elective courses for nursing students traditionally have come from disciplines that predominantly focus on the individual, such as psychology. Elective course offerings that emphasize the social context of health and health behaviours, such as sociology and anthropology, must be incorporated into curricula. In addition, students also need a sound knowledge of political systems and processes so that they can improve environments by meaningfully participating in social and governmental structures. Tenn and Niskala (1994) found Canadian schools of nursing had a limited emphasis in their curricula on the partnership role of the nurse in acting on the social determinants of health.

Second, students need to develop skills to collaborate with lay individuals and groups as well as with a variety of health and nonhealth professionals. The importance of collaboration with lay helpers is reflected in a conceptual framework for nursing education developed by Stewart (1990). Stewart found that most educational programs do not adequately develop the professional's skill in working with mutual aid and self-help groups. She advocates integrating social support theory into educational curricula to help professionals work with lay support groups.

In the area of nursing's collaboration with other professions, some have suggested that to facilitate harmonious working relationships among health professionals in intersectoral and interdisciplinary teams, students should be offered interdisciplinary courses in their undergraduate programs (CNA, 1988). This interdisciplinary education of health professionals, however, is not widespread in Canada, despite the success of pilot projects at McMaster, Manitoba, and other universities (CNA, 1988). Nurses continue to be educated for a single discipline.

To address some of these issues in their new undergraduate program, the University of Alberta Faculty of Nursing established an ad hoc committee on PHC and health promotion. This committee has representatives from the University of Alberta and the five collaborating diploma programs. The purpose of the committee is to ensure that PHC concepts are integrated into their 4-year program. Committee members monitor the curriculum and act as a resource for faculty members on PHC and health promotion principles. In addition, two interdisciplinary courses have been developed, one in international health and the other in ethics in health care.

The McGill Model of Nursing

To assist students in applying PHC principles in their practice, universities should select a nursing framework that incorporates the principles of PHC. Dr. Moira Allen and her colleagues at McGill University developed a Canadian nursing model that is consistent with some of the principles of primary health care (Allen, 1983; Gottlieb and Rowat, 1987). This model has been called the Allen Nursing Model (Kravitz and Frey, 1989) or the McGill Model (Gottlieb and Rowat, 1987).

Moira Allen (1983) argued that the most effective use of nursing skill was not in a replacement role for physicians in the provision of illness care but rather in a complementary role in which nurses focused on the health of families and individuals. Allen believed that the role of nursing was in the promotion of family health. The family was seen as the arena in which the individual learned how to maintain a healthy lifestyle. Unhealthy lifestyles already had been identified as the cause of much of the illness and disability in Canada (Lalonde, 1974).

Nurses who use this model in their practice will provide care that reflects some of the principles of PHC. First, the primary goal of the McGill model is health promotion. The role of the nurse is to help the individual or family to acquire healthy ways of living and to develop skills in problem-solving and coping. Although the definition of health in the McGill model is not as broad as the concept of health in primary health care, the McGill model shares the emphasis on health care that is preventive or promotive rather than curative only.

Second, in the McGill model, the family is seen as actively involved in seeking better health for its members and achieving life goals. The role of the nurse is that of a collaborator with the family. Rather than choosing or designing care for the family and the individual, the nurse works with the family to choose goals and select approaches to care. One of the principles of PHC is an emphasis on the active collaboration of the public with professionals in planning health services for communities. Nurses who work with families using the McGill model apply this principle at the individual and family care level. As families are helped by nurses to become more skilled in problem solving, to develop improved coping skills, and to live more healthy lives, they also become more able to participate in community involvement in health-care planning.

Because this model addresses both health and illness through a health-promotion focus, it has the potential to be used in acute-care settings. The nurse and the family focus on health by assessing how the family is coping with the illness of an individual. Together they determine how the nurse could help the family to increase their skill in problem solving and thus improve their coping.

The McGill model places less emphasis on the social and economic determinants of health than the concept of PHC. One of the principles of primary health care is the relationship of health to social and economic development. The environment in the McGill model refers to the settings in which the family can learn: the home, the community, the workplace, and health-care agencies. The role of the nurse is to construct environments in which clients can learn to access information and resources. In this model, the environment is the immediate circumstances or psychosocial environment of the family. Many family health problems, the lack of problem-solving skills, and the poor coping skills result from environmental conditions such as racism, poverty, violence, and pollution. Nursing models such as the McGill model generally have focused on an environmental paradigm that is client-oriented and psychosocial (Kleffel, 1991).

The McGill model evolved from descriptive studies of families in a variety of clinical settings. The goal of the model was to serve as a means of learning about nursing; Moira Allen expected the model to continue to develop based on research on the practice of nurses (Gottlieb and Rowat, 1987). Nurses may expand the McGill model of nursing to address environmental conditions that prevent families from learning problem-solving skills and improving their coping skills. As nurses become more involved in primary health care, the concept of the enviroment in this model may expand to include the role of the nurse in working with families to identify and address the factors in their environment that inhibit healthy living.

In summary, PHC is growing as a means of providing universally accessible health care to Canadians. Nursing associations and nurses are using PHC principles to develop a variety of services that provide nursing care. Despite the level of interest among nurses in providing PHC services, several issues remain: the need to remove financial barriers that prevent families from accessing health care, the need for health-care planners to define essential health-care services, the need to determine which health-care professionals are the appropriate source of care, the need to support a definition of health that includes economic and social conditions, and the need to develop collaboration among health disciplines and other sectors of the community. Nurses in practice and nursing educators have recognized the accompanying need for changes in the education of students and practitioners. Researchers are studying PHC principles in nursing education, and some educators have changed their curricula. With the continuing pressures on our health-care system, it is reasonable to expect further change in nursing practice and education.

■ REFERENCES

Alberta Association of Registered Nurses. (1993). *Nurses: Key to healthy Albertans*. Edmonton, Alberta: the Association.

Allen, M. (1983). Primary care nursing: Research in action. In L. Hockey (Ed.). *Primary care nursing* (pp. 32-77). Edinburgh: Churchill Livingstone.

Blackburn, C. (1991). *Poverty and health: Working with families*. Milton Keynes: Open University Press.

Boyle-McCauley Health Centre. (1993). *Annual update*. Edmonton: the Centre.

Butterfield, P. (1990). Thinking upstream: Nurturing a conceptual understanding of the societal context of health behavior. *Advances in Nursing Science, 12*(2), 1-8.

Canadian Nurses Association. (1988). *Health care for all Canadians: A call for health-care reform*. Ottawa: the Association.

Canadian Nurses Association. (1989). *Position statement on primary health care*. Ottawa: the Association.

Canadian Nurses Association. (Nov./Dec. 1992). *CNA Today*. Ottawa: the Association.

Canadian Nurses Association. (May 1993). *CNA Today*. Ottawa: the Association.

Canadian Nurses Association. (August 1993). *CNA Today*. Ottawa: the Association.

Canadian Public Health Association. (1989). *Position paper on health public policy: A framework*. Ottawa: the Association.

Canadian Public Health Association. (1990). *Position paper on sustainability and equity: Primary health care in developing countries*. Ottawa: the Association.

Chalmers, K., & Kristjanson, L. (1989). The theoretical basis for nursing at the community level: A comparison of three models. *Journal of Advanced Nursing, 14*, 569-574.

Dreher, M. (1982). The conflict of conservatism in public health nursing education. *Nursing Outlook, 30*, 504-509.

Edwards, N.C., & Craig, H. (1987). *Does nursing education reflect the goals of primary health care?* Hamilton, ON: McMaster University.

Epp, J. (1986). *Achieving health for all: A health promotion framework*. Ottawa: Health and Welfare Canada.

Family Service Association of Edmonton and the Income Security Action Committee. (1991). *Working hard, living lean*. Edmonton: the Committee.

Gottlieb, L. & Rowat, K. (1987). The McGill model of nursing: A practice-derived model. *Advances in Nursing Science, 9*(4), 51-61.

Health and Welfare Canada, Stephens, T., & Fowler, G.D. (Eds.) (1993), *Canada's Health Promotion Survey 1990: Technical Report.* Ottawa: Minister of Supply and Services, Canada.

Innes, J. (1987). Health care reform: sketching the future. *AARN Newsletter, 43*(8), 1, 5-6.

Jones, P., & Craig, D. (1988). Nursing practice in the community: Primary health care. In A. Baumgart & J. Larsen (Eds.), *Canadian nursing faces the future* (pp. 135-149). Toronto: Mosby.

Kaplan-Sanoff, M., Parker, S., & Zuckerman, B. (1991). Poverty and early childhood development: What do we know, and what should we do? *Infants and Young Children, 4*(1), 68-76.

Kleffel, D. (1991). Rethinking the environment as a domain of nursing knowledge. *Advances in Nursing Science, 14*(1), 40-51.

Kravitz, M. & Frey, M.A. (1989). The Allen nursing model. In J. Fitzpatrick & A. Whall (Eds.), *Conceptual models of nursing analysis and application.* (ed. 2) (pp. 313-329). East Norwalk, CT: Appleton & Lange.

Krebs, D. (1983). Nursing in primary health care. *International Nursing Review, 30*(5), 141-145.

Kristjanson, L.J., & Chalmers, K. (1991). Preventive work with families: Issues facing public health nurses. *Journal of Advanced Nursing, 16,* 147-153.

Lalonde, M. (1974). *A new perspective on the health of Canadians.* Ottawa: Government of Canada.

Mills, K., & Ready, H. (1988). Health promotion in community nursing practice. In A. Baumgart & J. Larsen (Eds.), *Canadian nursing faces the future* (pp. 151-161). Toronto: Mosby.

Neuman, B. (1989). *The Neuman systems model* (ed. 2). Norfolk, CT: Appleton & Lange.

Orem, D. (1985). *Nursing: Concepts of practice* (ed. 3). Toronto: McGraw Hill.

Parent, K. (1993). The launch of the Cheticamp Primary Health Care Project. *Nurse to Nurse, 4*(1), 20-21.

Pesznecker, B., Zerwekh, R., & Horn, B. (1989). The mutual-participation relationship: Key to facilitating self-care practices in clients and families. *Public Health Nursing, 6,* 197-203.

Premier's Commission on Future Health Care for Albertans. (1989). *The Rainbow Report: Our vision for health.* Edmonton: the commission.

Registered Nurses Association of British Columbia. (1990a). *Primary health care: A discussion paper.* Vancouver: the association.

Registered Nurses Association of British Columbia. (1990b). *Submission to the Royal Commission on Health Care and Costs.* Vancouver: the association.

Shestowsky, B. (1992). *Traditional medicine and primary health care among Canadian aboriginal people.* Ottawa: Aboriginal Nurses Association of Canada.

Stewart, M. J. (1989). Nurses' preparedness for health promotion through linkage with mutual-aid self-help groups. *Canadian Journal of Public Health, 80,* 110-114.

Stewart, M. J. (1990). From provider to partner: A conceptual framework for nursing education based on primary health care premises. *Advances in Nursing Science, 12*(2), 9-27.

Stevens, P., & Hall, J. (1992). Applying critical theories to nursing in communities. *Public Health Nursing, 9,* 2-9.

Tenn, L., & Niskala, H. (1994). *Primary health care in the curricula of Canadian university schools of nursing.* Final report to the Canadian Nurses Foundation. Vancouver, British Columbia: University of British Columbia.

Victorian Order of Nurses for Canada. (1992a). *Caring for life: Annual report 1991-92.* Ottawa: VON Canada.

Victorian Order of Nurses for Canada. (1992b). *VON Canada Report. Fall/Winter 1992.* Ottawa: the order.

Wilkins, R. (1988). *Special study on the socially and economically disadvantaged.* Ottawa: Minister of Supply and Services, Canada.

Working Group of Federal/Provincial/Territorial Nursing Consultants. (1991). *Report of the working group on the educational requirements of community health nurses.* Ottawa: Health and Welfare.

World Health Organization. (1978). *Primary health care: Report of the International Conference on Primary Health Care.* Alma Ata, USSR, Geneva: World Health Organization.

World Health Organization. (1984). *Health promotion: A discussion document on the concept and principles.* Copenhagen: Regional Office for the World Health Organization.

World Health Organization. (1988). *Alma Ata reaffirmed at Riga.* Riga, USSR, Geneva: World Health Organization.

6

NURSING RESEARCH AS A BASIS FOR PRACTICE IN CANADA

JANNETTA MACPHAIL

In the past decade nursing journals and conferences have placed increased emphasis on clinical nursing research and the importance of strengthening the research base of nursing practice. Nursing research journals have been urged to include utilization of research findings as well as the usual reporting of research methods, findings, and implications for practice. Indeed, in 1992 a new nursing research journal, *Clinical Nursing Research*, was launched by Wood and Hayes at the University of Alberta with a clearly international perspective. What are the reasons for such an increased focus on clinical research and the application of research findings in nursing practice? What are some of the facilitators and the deterrents of clinical research? What can practising nurses do to promote and support research? These are some of the questions to be addressed in this chapter.

▓ Research-Based Nursing Practice

Research-based nursing practice is simply practice based on valid and reliable research findings obtained from scientific investigation of nursing practice problems. Much of nursing practice today still is based on knowledge derived from trial-and-error experience or opinions and methods passed from generation to generation through books, articles, papers, conferences, workshops, and even through educational programs preparing students for entry to nursing practice. Nonetheless, an increasing proportion of nurses recognize the importance of research and research-based practice and are developing skills for critically evaluating research reports that are relevant to their practice. Johnson (1979, p. 1) states: "Research as a basis for practice, is increasingly necessary as a professional nurse becomes less content with past reliance on instinct and tradition and wants hard data for planning nursing care."

The focus of nursing practice is helping people, whether sick or well, to attain, maintain, or regain their optimal level of health and functioning. Nursing practice includes health assessment and health promotion and encompasses a variety of strategies or interventions, such as comfort measures, teaching, anticipatory guidance, support, and compensatory activities. Compensatory activities are actions taken by the nurse to compensate for what the patient cannot or will not do for himself or herself. They may include such activities as suctioning to maintain a clear airway, which is essential to respiration; assisting with ambulation to maintain circulation and joint and muscle function; and assisting with feeding to maintain nutritional status and elimination. All such strategies are designed to enhance the individual's health-seeking behaviours; to stimulate avoidance of disease and disability; to promote maximum use of the person's own resources in coping with disease or dysfunction; and to help the person cope with family responsibilities and crises.

The nature of nursing practice requires nurses to study individual and group behaviour in relation to attaining, maintaining, and regaining health. To develop a scientific base for nursing practice, the focus of research is on people's behaviour pertaining to motivation to be healthy, as well as their behaviour in coping with life crises. Life crises include such normal events as birth, developmental stages, and decline, as well as genetic failure, disease, and disability. Nursing research also may include behavioural responses to a wide variety of diagnostic and therapeutic interventions ordered by physicians. The feature that distinguishes nursing research from other research about human beings is the type of knowledge about people that nurses need and use in practice. Consequently, nursing research to advance knowledge and improve practice focuses on people's behaviour in response to circumstances that require nursing actions and their behaviour in response to that action (Schlotfeldt, 1971).

■ Clinical Nursing Research

An example of clinical nursing research designed to answer practical questions of practising nurses is Day's study to develop and evaluate a program designed to teach handicapped grade-one children about hand-washing in the prevention and control of contagious diseases, such as colds, flu, and ear infections. Children in the study were taught when and how to wash their hands. Hand-washing skills and frequency were evaluated at 1, 3, and 6 months after teaching and were found to improve. The children had fewer visits to the doctor, took fewer prescribed medications, and had fewer illnesses than in the same period during the previous year. An interesting result of the study was that the children challenged the nurses about their hand-washing techniques with comments such as, "You can't touch me. I saw you blow your nose. Go and wash your hands first" (AFNR Annual Report, 1989-1990).

Other examples of practical research are studies of pain control. Duggleby questioned hospital policy that prevented elderly patients from administering their own analgesics to control pain because physicians and nurses thought they would not be able to manage the technology that regulates dosage. Her study assessed elderly patients' ability to use this effective method of pain control and found the health care providers' fears to be groundless. The outcome was a change in hospital policy (*AFNR* Annual Report, 1990-1991). In investigating the use of transcutaneous electrical nerve stimulation (TENS) for pain control for thoracotomy patients, Finlay found that "patients were generally given too little pain medication and that the use of TENS was generally ineffective in relieving pain under these circumstances" (*AFNR* Annual Report, 1990-1991, p. 7). McQueen's interest in finding a site for the administration of intramuscular injections less painful than the usual site in the buttocks also resulted in a change in practice. Through her research she found that "a site higher up caused less pain and was associated with fewer complications" (*AFNR* Annual Report, 1990-1991, p. 7).

Researchers conducted a follow-up study of day-surgery patients because nursing staff members were concerned that information given to patients was inadequate and that the stressful situation was not conducive to learning. Oberle, Allen, and Lynkowski translated the nurses' concerns into a questionnaire and conducted telephone interviews with 270 patients on the fourth postoperative day. They found that many patients had knowledge gaps and were not prepared for the resulting pain, degree of disability, fatigue, and inability to meet work and home commitments. The nursing staff used the findings to change their teaching and follow-up care to overcome the inadequacies. This is an example of how the collaborative efforts of nursing staff and researchers can improve practice (*AFNR* Annual Report, 1991-1992).

Hawthorne (1994) investigated whether perceptions of coronary artery bypass surgery differ between women and men and whether such differences influence recovery. She found that the surgery may be more disruptive for men than women because they experience it 10 to 20 years earlier than women and in their peak earning years. The major differences found in recovery were that almost all men participated in the rehabilitation program but few women did, and "women deferred the monitoring of their cardiac risk factors to their physician, whereas men tended to follow their own numbers' religiously" (Hawthorne, 1994, p. 79). Men followed specific discharge guidelines when resuming activities, whereas women used family and home responsibilities and level of fatigue as their activity and rehabilitation guides. The data suggest that women may have less time available to participate in rehabilitation and risk-factor reduction programs. Hawthorne also found differences in communication styles, with men communicating much more readily with physicians and other providers than women, who tended to be passive and defer to the predominantly male physicians. This could have an adverse effect on the sharing of critical information and the treatment and rehabilitation plans for women. There is need for further investigation of gender differences because women were not included in research on cardiac disease until very recently. Many other examples could be cited of research questions arising from practice and of research findings leading to changes in practice. In the past 2 decades, particularly the nursing research literature and nursing specialty clinical journals have included reports of clinically oriented research and implications for change in nursing practice; however, the outcomes in terms of effecting changes are not known.

Research-based practice has become even more important with diminishing health care funds. The nursing profession must demonstrate how nursing interventions make a difference in improving the health status and health potential of individuals, families, and communities. The only way this can be accomplished is through research followed by the dissemination of findings to be applied in practice. The nursing profession must move much more rapidly than in the past to research-based practice, which is a challenge as funding for both health care and research decreases. What has deterred nursing from increasing its research base? What can nurses do to promote and facilitate research-based practice?

■ Deterrents to Research-Based Nursing Practice

One of the major deterrents to research-based nursing practice has been the limited number of nurses prepared to conduct research. Although the number of nurses prepared at the master's and doctoral levels has increased considerably in the past decade in Canada and the United States, the proportion of nurses actually conducting research to strengthen the scientific base of practice is still limited. The number of nurses holding an earned doctorate in Canada increased from 81 in 1980 to 124 in 1982, to 193 in 1986, and to 257 in 1989, and the number of nurses involved in doctoral preparation increased from 72 in 1980 to 121 in 1982, to 224 in 1986, and to 265 in 1989 (Stinson, Larsen, and MacPhail, 1984; Stinson, MacPhail, and Larsen, 1988; Lamb and Stinson, 1990). Thus the number of nurses with an earned doctorate increased by 53% from 1980 to 1982, by 56% from 1982 to 1986, and by 33% from 1986 to 1989; and the number of nurses engaged in doctoral study increased by 68% from 1980 to 1982, by 85% from 1982 to 1986, and by 18% from 1986 to 1989. The reasons for recent decreases in both categories are not known but may be related to insufficient funding for graduate study and the lack of nursing doctoral programs in Canada until 1991. The establishment of five doctoral programs in nursing (University of Alberta, January 1991; University of British Columbia, September 1991; University of Toronto, September 1993; a joint doctoral program by McGill University and l'Université de Montréal, September 1993; and McMaster University, 1994) should help to increase the number of Canadian nurses pursuing doctoral education. Also needed are more funds for doctoral study, which is problematic with the cutbacks in funding for both health care and education in the provinces.

A second deterrent to conducting research in practice is the difficulty in asking the research question, which is the most complex and the most important task of any researcher. Although research can solve problems, not all problems are research questions. The question, "Why don't staff nurses use the medication cart as it was designed?" reflects a problem. It may imply the question of how to get them to do it. The problem may be a management or morale problem, but as stated, it is not a research problem (Ellis, 1974). Two major types of questions are not researchable. These are value or "should" questions and "yes" or "no" questions. Types of researchable questions as identified by Wilson (1985, p. 117) are:

1. Why are things this way? For example, why do cancer patients without hope participate in painful experiments?
2. What would happen if? For example, what would happen if sex education were taught in all schools?
3. Which approach would work better? For example, is group or individual counselling more effective with clients who abuse alcohol?
4. Who might benefit from this? For example, would hospitalized children have faster recoveries if parents were permitted and taught to participate in their care?

Dickoff, James, and Wiedenbach (1968, p. 420) developed another categorization of types of research questions:

1. Factor-isolating or "naming." For example, what are the stages of the grieving process?
2. Factor-relating or "what is happening here?" For example, what is the relationship of parents' own childhood experiences to their engaging in subsequent child abuse or neglect?
3. Situation-relating or "what will happen?" For example, will feedback training decrease suffering among chronic pain patients?
4. Situation-producing or "how can I make it happen?" For example, how can I intervene to prevent postoperative vomiting?

Brink and Wood (1983) define a researchable question as one that yields problem-solving information, produces new research, adds to theory, or improves practice. Lindeman and Schantz (1982) define it more narrowly as a question that can be answered by collecting observable data, that includes reference to the relationship between two or more variables, and that emanates from what is known about phenomena.

Defining researchable questions requires time and thought and a thorough search of literature to determine what is known about the phenomenon being considered. Only in this way can one decide whether a question is worth investigating. Other factors that affect the feasibility of studying the question are time, availability of subjects, cooperation of others, facilities and equipment, money, research experience, and ethical considerations.

Many authors have indentified insufficient time as an impediment to conducting research. It is a concern of faculty members who devote much time to teaching, curriculum development, committee work, and professional activities. Time for research may be limited by the orientation in nursing to "doing" and "being busy" and a tendency to want immediate results. Several writers have reported that nurses tend to want immediate results and fast action and have difficulty understanding that a hunch may not be borne out by research. On the other hand, educators may have difficulty using their time for research when they are accustomed to devoting it to teaching, curriculum study and revision, and committee work. This might also be related to lagging commitment to research, as termed by Werley (1972).

Another deterrent to research in practice may be lack of access to patients. Access may be limited by physicians who have certain prerogatives with their patients, whether hospitalized, in clinics, or in offices. Access also may be limited by nurses who do not support or understand nursing research; nurses are in key positions to influence physicians, other nurses, and patients by educating them about the importance of research in nursing practice. This is not to suggest that patients' rights should not be protected, or that research proposals should not be subject to rigorous review for ethics and quality. Rather, it is to urge nurses to think about their influence on access to patients and the promotion of nursing research.

Insufficient funds to support research is an obstacle for all types of nursing research. It is a major problem in Canada because separate funding for nursing research has never been provided on the federal level, as in the United States, where it has helped researchers gain experience in research design and grant-writing needed to be able to compete in the larger arena (Gortner, 1986). On the federal level, the Canadian government provides research funds for the social sciences and humanities, for the natural sciences and engineering, and for medicine and other health-related disciplines. Medical Research Council (MRC) funds are supposed to be available to health sciences other than medicine; however, most have been awarded to medicine. After vigorous lobbying by the Canadian Nurse Association (CNA) and the Canadian Association of University Schools of Nursing (CAUSN) for a number of years for representation on the MRC, nursing finally succeeded in having a nurse appointed in 1986. Despite success in obtaining some modifications in funding policies for nursing research, a very limited proportion of MRC funding has been awarded to nurse investigators to date. The National Health Research and Development Program (NHRDP)-MRC Joint Program in Nursing was developed a number of years ago to assist the nursing profession in establishing research in university faculties of nursing. In the past 7 years the positions of six nursing scientists in several universities were funded to allow them to focus on research. Recently in the final competition in this Joint Program, the positions of six additional nursing scientists in three universities (University of Alberta, l'Université de Montréal, and University of Toronto) were funded to permit them not only to focus on research but also to assist nursing colleagues to undertake research as well. One of the nursing scientists at the University of Alberta also was awarded an operating grant to support her research project, the first such grant to be awarded under the Program.

Other research funding available to nurse researchers is limited. Since 1985 the Canadian Nurses Foundation (CNF) has offered small research grants, initially $2500 and increased to a maximum of $5000 in 1993. Two special grant categories were established with special funding in 1990, one for $15,000 in primary health care research and the other for $10,000 for pharmaceutical-related research. Through fund-raising efforts of the CNF, two more $15,000 research grants became available in 1994 for research in any area of nursing practice (personal communication with Beverly Campbell, executive director of CNF, November 8, 1993). Although the grants available from CNF still are relatively small, there is evidence of progress in the number of grant proposals received and the total amount of funds awarded annually: $9602 in 1989; $21,582 in 1990; $37,500 in 1991; and $75,823 in 1992. The number of grant proposals received increased from 23 in 1990 to 33 in 1992, and the number of grants awarded increased from 7 in 1990 to 15 in 1992 (CNF Annual Reports, 1990 and 1992).

Research funds also may be available through provincial nursing associations, but the amounts tend to be even smaller. A few nurse researchers have been awarded "Career Scientist" grants by the Ontario Ministry of Health and the Research Division of the British Columbia Children's Hospital, which require that the recipients devote 75% of their time to research and other scholarly activities. Nurses also may apply for research funding through disease-oriented specialty organizations, such as heart, lung, diabetes, and cancer organizations, but they are competing with medicine and other health disciplines.

Another source of research funding for nursing became available in 1982 when the Alberta Foundation for Nursing Research was established by ministerial order as a response to lobbying by the Alberta Association of Registered Nurses (AARN) and nursing leaders of the University of Alberta and the University of Calgary. A fund of $1 million was allocated for use over a 5-year period, and a board of directors was appointed to establish research categories, guidelines, and a review process, and to award and administer the funds. Support services to administer the fund were provided by the Alberta Department of Advanced Education. At the end of the 5 years, negotiations and political pressure succeeded in obtaining another $1 million for a 5-year period (to 1993). The first awards were made in the 1983-1984 fiscal year, and a total of $2,163,806 was awarded to Alberta nurses by the end of the 1991-1992 fiscal year. The amounts awarded per year and the number of awards made reflect remarkable progress, as shown by the allocation of $19,015 to 7 recipients in the first year (1983-1984); $280,404 for 33 awards in 1988 to 1989; $392,675 for 29 awards in 1990 to 1991; and $314,499 for 26 awards in 1991 to 1992 (Alberta Foundation for Nursing Research, 1990-1991, and AFNR, 1991-1992). In some grant categories, the amounts available were increased as new ideas evolved and experience showed that original amounts were insufficient to achieve the research objectives. For example, the maximum award for the "Research Project" category was increased from $25,000 to $50,000 and then to $85,000; and the maximum duration was increased from 2 to 3 years in the 1989-1990 fiscal year (AFNR, 1989-1990).

In addition to having a significant effect on the development of nursing research in Alberta, the AFNR has helped to increase the visibility of Alberta nurse researchers, as many AFNR-funded studies have been published and presented at national and international research conferences. With the establishment of the AFNR, Alberta became the first and only province or state worldwide to designate funds exclusively for nursing research. It is also the first research funding endeavour in Canada in which nurses have had a primary role in reviewing grant proposals and awarding funds. Sadly, with recent cutbacks in funding for research, education, and health care by the Alberta Legislature the future of the AFNR is tenuous as originally structured. Nurses in Alberta are working toward the development of a new structure, which would continue to support funding for nursing research. This structure would amalgamate the efforts of the AARN, the Alberta Nurses Educational Trust, and the present arrangement for AFNR. It remains to be seen how this initiative will develop in the future.

A final deterrent to achieving the goal of research-based practice pertains to the utilization of research findings in practice settings. Since such a limited proportion of nurses are prepared to conduct research and interpret research findings, there is need for intermediary mechanisms to assist nursing staff in interpreting and applying research findings in practice. There is also need for changes in values and incentives to recognize and reward research-based nursing practice. McClure (1981) has noted that to support research, a nurse executive requires a substantial knowledge of research methods and research literature, not only to provide a climate that supports research, but also to guide a study through various review committees and to make the arrangements necessary for investigations to proceed. She believes that commitment of time and energy by the nurse executive is essential to promoting and facilitating research and applying research findings in practice.

■ Strategies to Promote Research and Research-Based Practice

The deterrents identified in relation to the development of research and the promotion of research-based practice in themselves suggest possible solutions. Implementation of solutions or strategies will require strong commitment and determination by all nurses, not just nurses involved in research or who want to conduct research.

A basic requirement is to increase the proportion of nurses who appreciate the importance of research, understand research methods, and have a beginning ability to evaluate research reports critically. This implies a need for more baccalaureate-prepared nurses, which is in line with our profession's goal for entry to practice by the year 2000. Remarkable progress has been made within the past 3 years, particularly, in developing collaborative programs between university faculties/schools of nursing and diploma programs in the western provinces and the Atlantic region provinces designed to increase greatly opportunities for baccalaureate education in nursing. (Some of the collaborative efforts are described in Chapter 6.)

A second strategy is to increase the proportion of nurses prepared at the master's and doctoral levels. More funding is needed to increase enrollments, for which all nurses should lobby. Some nursing faculty members have competed successfully for funds to support research training and research projects; however, the number has been small and the proportion almost infinitesimal when compared with funding for medicine and other disciplines. In addition to increasing enrollments, attention must be given to the quality of the research preparation within graduate programs, to providing resources for faculty to increase research competence and grantsmanship skills, and to holding faculty members accountable for conducting research and disseminating their findings.

The Canadian Nurses Association (CNA) has been a strong proponent of nursing research, particularly since the 1960s. The CNA Board allocated $10,000 to support the establishment of the Canadian Nurses Foundation (CNF) in 1962 to serve as a mechanism to receive funds and award them on a competitive basis to nurses admitted to baccalaureate and graduate programs. Funds are raised through membership dues and appeals for donations to individuals, associations, and corporations. In 1984 the CNF added a small research grants program up to $2,500, which was increased to a maximum of $5,000 in 1993. Although the available funds do not meet all the needs, the CNF plays an important role in encouraging nurses to pursue baccalaureate and graduate education, and to undertake small research projects, and develop grant-writing skills. Other examples of the CNA's support of nursing research are the following: (1) establishment of a nursing research committee in 1971 that became a standing committee in 1978; (2) amendment of CNA bylaws in 1976 to include a member-at-large for nursing research on the board of directors; (3) publication of the first inventory of Canadian nursing doctoral statistics in 1980, with updates in 1982, 1986, and 1989; (4) publication of the CNA's *Research Imperative for Nursing in Canada,* a strategic plan for the development of nursing research prepared by the research committee, approved by the board of directors in 1984, and revised in 1990; and (5) vigorous lobbying over the years for recognition and funding of nursing research and graduate education to prepare more nurses to conduct research.

Many strategies to create a climate supporting research in practice settings and to promote research-based practice have been effective. One is the appointment of a clinical nurse researcher who works with the nursing staff to formulate research questions, who designs and conducts research projects, and who involves staff members in the process. The role includes educating staff members about nursing research and its importance and potential for improving practice, and establishing a proper research-review process for screening nursing research proposals before they are sent to the institutional review committee. The researcher may be in a joint appointment with the cost shared by the health-care agency and a university faculty/school of nursing. This approach has been applied effectively by a number of universities (Alberta, British Columbia, Calgary, Dalhousie, Manitoba, McGill, McMaster, Ottawa, and Toronto) in collaboration with hospitals and other health-care agencies. The role also includes interpreting nursing research to other disciplines, notably medicine; serving on the institutional research-review committee; ensuring that the research-review process is rigorous; and assisting in the application of valid and reliable research findings. The enactment of such a role requires a nurse prepared at the doctoral level who is not only competent in designing and conducting research, but also skilled in communication and in effecting planned change. It also requires strong administrative support, ability to create a research climate that encourages questioning current practices, readiness to test different nursing approaches, and nursing staff interested in trying new approaches.

The provision of research consultation is another strategy found to be effective in promoting quality research and research-based practice. Also important are library resources, educationally prepared nurses, funding, and time to be involved in research endeavours (Thurston, Tenove, and Church, 1990; Fitch, 1992; Rosswurm, 1992). Research consultation has been provided to Saskatchewan nurses through the Saskatchewan Nursing Research Unit, established in 1983 with joint sponsorship by the University of Saskatchewan College of Nursing, the Saskatchewan Registered Nurses Association, and the Saskatchewan Union of Nurses. Similar services have been provided by the Manitoba Nursing Research Unit, funded jointly by the University of Manitoba School of Nursing and the Manitoba Association of Registered Nurses beginning in 1985; and to nurses in all parts of Alberta for 1 year (1986-1987) through a special grant that supported a nursing research consultant and was administered through the Alberta Foundation for Nursing Research. All these programs demonstrated the need for this type of service to increase and enhance research. In the first 6 months, research consultation was provided to more than 100 nurses in Alberta; 35% were from hospitals and nursing homes, 26% from colleges and universities, and 12% from professional associations and committees (AFNR, 1987). The response was gratifying and clearly reflected a great need for research consultation in Alberta. This need continues, as identified by the AFNR board of directors, who requested the Alberta Association of Registered Nurses (AARN) "to explore the possibility of creating a Nursing Research Consultant position" (*AFNR Annual Report*, 1990-1991, p. 2). Such a position was established by the Registered Nurses Association of British Columbia in 1988, and Dr. Heather Clarke clearly demonstrated the potential and feasibility of the role in that province. Fiscal restraints have precluded its development in Alberta, where universities continue to provide some consultation through joint appointees and other collaborative endeavours; however, this does not meet all of the identified needs in that province.

Pepler (1992) describes the strategies used in a major teaching hospital to promote research-based practice. As a nursing-research consultant in that setting, she developed a 24-hour educational program presented over a 12-week period that is available to nursing staff from other hospitals in Montreal as well as to the Royal Victoria Hospital staff. It has "helped nurses gain the knowledge and skills to find, interpret and judge research findings and to change their world of practice" (Pepler, 1992, p. 27). Other reported outcomes are greater use of research consultation services, ability to understand research presentations at conferences, and increased support for nursing research and research-based practice.

Unit-based research roundtable discussions, undertaken jointly by faculty and unit leaders, are another approach to increase awareness of the relevance of research to practice and to disseminate research findings to nursing staff and nursing students (Janken, Dufault, and Yeaw, 1988). Although the process required time, patience, and persistence, they found it resulted in more favourable attitudes toward research, increased application of research findings in practice, improved communications, and the development of a new respect between staff and students.

A strategy tried by some nurse researchers is to provide an interpretation of research findings in language that nursing staff can understand. Kirchhoff (1983) favours this approach by providing summaries of results in clinically oriented journals; however, the summaries must be written by a competent researcher. The American Association of Critical Care Nurses has used this approach in their clinical journal, *Focus*, by including reviews of nursing studies with suggestions for practice. The *Western Journal of Nursing Research* used a similar strategy by publishing a column, "Using Research in Practice." Haller, Reynolds, and Horsley (1979) used research-based protocols for nursing staff to follow in several Michigan hospitals as another approach to promoting research-based practice. It is essential to have a scholarly critique of the original research and ensure that nursing staff members and students recognize that such protocols and suggestions for practice cannot be applied without the interim step of interpretation by a skilled researcher. Kirchhoff (1983) also suggests that research conferences include a response to a research report titled "Clinical Application," presented by a skilled researcher-clinician. Such an approach might encourage more nursing staff members to attend research conferences.

Another strategy to stimulate the development of research and research-based practice is to organize research interest groups within the professional organization or within a health-care agency or group of agencies. Such a group requires a leader with research expertise to help the group define its purposes. Is it to learn to read and apply research findings, to conduct research, or both? Should there be one general research group, or should there be smaller groups focused on particular clinical interests? Experience with such interest groups has demonstrated great potential when leadership is provided by nurses knowledgeable about research methods and able to help the group identify researchable practice problems. Other approaches used in health-care agencies are organizing research rounds, holding research presentations over lunch hour, and forming journal clubs in which research discussion is led by a competent investigator. Another technique is to involve staff in data collection so they learn what is involved in research and that research results are not immediately forthcoming.

Staff participation in research review and ethical clearance can be a valuable learning opportunity if under the direction and guidance of a competent nurse researcher who works with the staff to help them understand all the factors that must be considered. One must assess the quality of a research proposal in order to give ethical clearance; if the study is not well designed it is not ethical to take the patients' or subjects' time. This implies that the nurse researcher must select a committee and educate the members about the review process. They need basic knowledge of research and the requirements for reviewing and interpreting nursing research, which implies that members have at least a baccalaureate degree. Guidelines for research review have been developed in some health-care agencies, such as the University of Alberta Hospitals, where a clinical nurse researcher provided leadership in the process. These guidelines are available to nurses involved or interested in promoting and facilitating research in other agencies.

Researchers can share their findings through written media as well as verbal presentations. Findings can be published in the health-care agency's monthly newsletter. Some nursing departments have a publication of some type in which a column can be devoted to research. Professional association newsletters have included such a column to reach more nurses. Both should be done under the guidance of a competent researcher to ensure that quality is maintained and that terminology is appropriate for neophytes in research.

In the process of learning about nursing research, nursing staff members and students become familiar with nursing research journals. These include *Nursing Research, Research in Nursing and Health, Advances in Nursing Science, Image: Journal of Nursing Scholarship, Western Journal of Nursing Research*, and *Clinical Nursing Research: An International Journal*. All are published in the United States, but since 1987 the *Western Journal of Nursing Research* has been edited at the University of Alberta by Pamela Brink and Marilynn Wood of the Faculty of Nursing. *Clinical Nursing Research* is a journal launched in 1992 to focus on clinical practice problems, encourage discussion among practitioners, identify potential clinical application of the latest scholarly research, and disseminate research findings of particular interest to practising nurses. It is edited at the University of Alberta by Marilynn Wood and Pat Hayes. The *Canadian Journal of Nursing Research* (formerly *Nursing Papers*) is the only Canadian nursing research journal. It has been edited and published through McGill University since 1968. Its readership has been limited but is increasing gradually, with more doctorally prepared nurses conducting research and sharing their findings. Thus opportunities are increasing to publish nursing research, promote and facilitate the application of valid and reliable findings in practice, and progress toward the goal of research-based nursing practice.

■ The Future of Research-Based Nursing Practice

The progress made in increasing the number of nurses prepared to conduct research and the number and quality of practice-oriented studies undertaken by nurse researchers is encouraging. Nonetheless, practising nurses, as individuals and as members of their professional organization, need to promote and support the advancement of nursing knowledge through research, and improve nursing practice and health care through application of valid and reliable research findings. As we approach the twenty-first century with increasing competition for scarce financial resources, strong commitment to this goal will be required of all nurses-practitioners, educators, administrators, and researchers—to continue to strengthen the research base of nursing practice.

■ **REFERENCES**

Alberta Foundation for Nursing Research. (1986-1987). *Annual Report*. Edmonton, Alberta: the Foundation.

Alberta Foundation for Nursing Research. (1989-1990). *Annual Report*. Edmonton, Alberta: the Foundation.

Alberta Foundation for Nursing Research. (1990-1991). *Annual Report*. Edmonton, Alberta: the Foundation.

Alberta Foundation for Nursing Research. (1991-1992). *Annual Report*. Edmonton, Alberta: the Foundation.

Brink, P.J. and Wood, M.J. (1983). *Basic steps in planning nursing research: from question to proposal.* (ed. 2). Belmont, CA: Wadsworth Health Services.

Canadian Nurses Foundation. (1990). *1990 Annual Report*. Ottawa, Ontario: the foundation.

Canadian Nurses Foundation. (1992). *1992 Annual Report*. Ottawa, Ontario: the foundation.

Dickoff, J., James, P., & Wiedenbach, E. (1968). Theory in a practice discipline: Part I. Practice-oriented theory. *Nursing Research, 17*(5), 415-435.

Ellis, R. (1974). Asking the research question. In: *Issues in research: social, professional and methodological* (pp. 31-35). Kansas City, MO: American Nurses Association.

Fitch, M. (1992). Five years in the life of a nursing research and professional development division. *Canadian Journal of Nursing Administration, 5*(2), 20-26.

Gortner, S.R. (1986). Impact of the Division of Nursing on research development in the United States. In S.M. Stinson & J.C. Kerr (Eds.), *International issues in nursing research* (pp. 113-130). London: Croon Helm.

Haller, K.B., Reynolds, M.A., & Horsley, J.A. (1979). Developing research-based innovation protocols: Process, criteria and issues. *Research in Nursing and Health, 2*(2), 45-51.

Hawthorne, M.H. (1994). Gender differences in recovery after coronary artery surgery. *Image: Journal of Nursing Scholarship, 26*(1), 75-80.

Janken, J.K., Dufault, M.A., & Yeaw, E.M. (1988). Research round tables: Increasing student/staff awareness of the relevancy of research to practice. *Journal of Professional Nursing, 4*(3), 186-191.

Johnson, J.E. (1979). Translating research into practice. In: *Power nursing's challenge for change* (pp. 125-133). Kansas City, MO: American Nurses Association.

Kirchhoff, K.T. (1983). Using research in practice: Should staff nurses be expected to use research? *Western Journal of Nursing Research, 5*(3), 245-247.

Lamb, M.A., & Stinson, S.M. (1990). *Canadian nursing doctoral statistics: 1989 update*. Ottawa, Ontario: Canadian Nurses Association.

Lindeman, C.A., & Schantz, D. (1982). The research question. *Journal of Nursing Administration, 12*(1), 6-10.

McClure, M.L. (1981). Promoting practice-based research: A critical need. *Journal of Nursing Administration, 11*(11 & 12), 66-70.

Pepler, C. (1992). Fostering change through education. *The Canadian Nurse, 88*(1), 25-27.

Rosswurm, M.A. (1992). A research-based practice model in a hospital setting. *Journal of Nursing Administration, 22*(3), 57-59.

Schlotfeldt, R.M. (1971). The significance of empirical research for nursing. *Nursing Research, 20*(2), 140-142.

Stinson, S.M., Larsen, J., & MacPhail, J. (1984). *Canadian nursing doctoral statistics: 1982 update*. Ottawa, Ontario: Canadian Nurses Association.

Stinson, S.M., MacPhail, J., & Larsen, J. (1988). *Canadian nursing doctoral statistics: 1986 update*. Ottawa, Ontario: Canadian Nurses Association.

Thurston, N., Tenove, S., & Church, J. (1990). Hospital nursing research is alive and flourishing. *Nursing Management, 21*(5), 50-54.

Werley, H. (1972). This I believe about clinical nursing research. *Nursing Outlook, 20*(11), 718-722.

Wilson, H.S. (1985). *Research in Nursing*. Don Mills, Ontario: Addison-Wesley Publishing Company.

THE CHANGING FACE OF NURSING EDUCATION IN CANADA

JANET ROSS KERR AND JANNETTA MACPHAIL

■ Standards in Nursing Education: A Historical Perspective

Program quality has been an important concern since the first nursing education programs were developed in hospitals before the end of the last century. The system of nursing education that evolved placed a low priority on the education of women in society. To this day there are strong elements of a feminist struggle against traditional views on the education of women in the drive to improve standards and quality in nursing education. Nursing students were exploited in the apprenticeship system of nursing education that developed in hospital-based diploma nursing programs. Ending this exploitation and ensuring that the goal of nursing programs was the education of the student became causes championed by nursing educators over most of this century. In the 1920s and 1930s, nursing leaders argued for a standard curriculum and for allowing programs to be operated only by hospitals that had enough beds to ensure that schools had the clinical and material resources to support a strong nursing education program. In 1932, Dr. George Weir reported the results of the first national study of nursing education. This study was commissioned jointly by the Canadian Nurses Association (CNA) and the Canadian Medical Association and confirmed nursing educators' worst fears, that conditions in nursing schools were deplorable, that the health of students was being compromised, and that education was secondary to hospital service as a priority in the schools.

Preparing a sufficient number of graduate nurses became the rallying cry of the 1940s, both during the war and throughout the late 1940s and 1950s. In the expansionist years of the 1960s, nursing leaders called for better prepared faculty in schools and for quality and standards as priorities in nursing education programs. Existing nursing degree programs began to expand, and new programs emerged in other universities. The basic integrated degree model became the program of choice by the 1970s, as the Royal Commission on Health Services of 1964 castigated universities for granting degrees for work over which they had no control, namely the 3-year apprenticeship-based hospital diploma program that was "sandwiched" between 2 years of university study in most nonintegrated baccalaureate degree programs.

The demand for the transfer of responsibility for nursing education to the general educational system which had begun in earnest with the Weir Report of 1932, was heightened by experiments with 2-year programming in the 1950s, when the Demonstration School was established in association with the Metropolitan General Hospital in Windsor, Ontario. Made possible by a grant from the Canadian Red Cross Society, this experimental school was deemed successful in an evaluation of the project (Lord, 1952). The rallying cry of the reformists began to be heard in the 1960s, and the movement to separate nursing education programs from the authority of hospitals began in earnest. Two year programs in nursing began to appear and Ontario, Quebec, and Saskatchewan developed a system of diploma education based entirely in community colleges. This transfer of diploma programs to the general education system was in full swing when the Alberta Task Force on Nursing Education recommended in 1975 that all new graduates be prepared at the baccalaureate level before entering professional practice. The position was endorsed by the Alberta Association of Registered Nurses in 1976, and was approved by the CNA in 1982 with a target date of the year 2000. By 1988, when the New Brunswick Association of Registered Nurses endorsed the position, all provincial associations had declared their support (Canadian Nurses Association, September, 1991a).

The Entry-to-Practice Position (EP2000)

The entry-to-practice position stipulates that all new graduates in nursing must be qualified at the baccalaureate level when they enter the professional practice of nursing. The year 2000 was set as a goal for implementation. Although this position originally was offered by a government committee in Alberta, it became a highly valued goal of the nursing profession across the country in less than a decade. When nursing organizations put forward their statements supporting the position, they hoped that the position would become a reality by the expected date. Nurses realized from the outset, however, that the position would not be easily achieved, but neither did they believe that it was impossible. The position never has had any kind of legal or political mandate. The reluctance of provincial governments for 2 decades to endorse the baccalaureate standard for entry to the practice of nursing reflects the fact that equality in education for women is yet to be achieved. The announcement by Premier McKenna of New Brunswick in 1992 that the baccalaureate degree should be a prerequisite to the practice of nursing was the first such endorsement by a first minister of a Canadian province (Nurses Association of New Brunswick, 1992). This standard would not have been established in Prince Edward Island in 1992 without the strong support of the provincial government. Political support will be forthcoming gradually in other provinces as the nation edges toward achieving EP2000.

Progress in Achieving the Entry-to-Practice Position (EP2000)

In addition to the resolution passed at the 1980 CNA Biennial Convention in Vancouver requesting that the association study the feasibility of adopting a position favouring entry to practice, a paper entitled *Entry to the Practice of Nursing: A Background Paper* (1982) was developed, and in 1982 the association's board of directors approved the entry-to-practice position. The position also was endorsed unanimously by delegates attending the CNA Biennial Convention in Newfoundland in that year. After the CNA approved the position in 1982, the national organization set out to promote the entry-to-practice standard among its member associations. The fact that the vast majority of nurses were qualified at only the diploma level at the time the entry-to-practice position was put forward meant that a great deal of discussion and consideration would be necessary among nurses at every level throughout the country. It is one thing for a professional association to approve a position, but quite another for all members to understand, accept, and promote it.

The CNA established the position of entry-to-practice coordinator and for several years regularly sent *Entry to Practice* newsletters to all provinces. Beginning in 1991, *Edufacts*, the series of newsletters that followed, focused more broadly on issues in educational standards, including entry to practice. In these newsletters, the CNA set out the case for the baccalaureate standard and offered evidence for its acceptance. These newsletters provided the evidence and resource material for nurses at the provincial level to argue the case within their own membership, with government, and with the public. The carefully prepared background information presented in CNA publications assisted the provinces to develop rational and coherent strategies for implementing the EP2000 position in the regions of the country. It also created a national profile for the campaign to implement the entry-to-practice position.

British Columbia

To date, much progress has occurred in the west and in the east. In British Columbia, the 1989 merger between the University of British Columbia (UBC) School of Nursing and the School of Nursing at the Vancouver General Hospital (VGH) was the first formal step to forge a link between a diploma and a baccalaureate degree program in nursing. The new program first was offered in the fall of 1989, with the UBC program extended to the VGH site (CNA, 1993a). Since then, several developments have occurred in British Columbia. The University of Victoria (UVic) initially developed collaborative arrangements with several community colleges—Camosun, Cariboo, Malaspina, and Okanagan Colleges. Because Okanagan and Cariboo University colleges were expected to acquire degree-granting powers in the future, UVic and these institutions developed different arrangements. The university worked closely with college faculty who offered the courses throughout the 4 years to assist them in offering the courses for which UVic granted a baccalaureate degree in nursing. Although Malaspina College is also a university college, it initially participated by offering some post-RN courses. As there is now a proposal for Malaspina to offer the full program to both post-RN and continuing students, it seems likely that Malaspina will move into an arrangement similar to that the university has with Okanagan and Cariboo University colleges. UVic also has taken on some additional partners in its collaborative program—Langara College, North Island College (first students admitted September, 1993), and Selkirk College (first students admitted September, 1994). Two additional colleges, Douglas College and Kwantlen College in Vancouver, joined as collaborative partners and plan to admit their first students in September, 1996 (personal communication, Dr. Anita Molzahn, September 2, 1994). The collaborative initiatives at the basic integrated baccalaureate level were the logical extension of UVic's initial development of its post-RN program on the campuses of Okanagan and Cariboo colleges further to the 1987 provincial government resolution to increase access to postsecondary education.

Other developments in British Columbia have occurred at the newly established University of Northern British Columbia (UNBC). This institution began with a nursing program already in place that has collaborated with community colleges, including Northern Lights Community College and the College of New Caledonia. A third college, Northwest College, initially was a partner in this consortium but decided not to admit students to the collaborative program in September, 1994, as originally planned. However, the goal of participation in the program by Northwest College remained a possibility. A collaborative, 4-year curriculum was developed in a relatively short time because the three colleges already had a common curriculum and the college supported a move to a baccalaureate curriculum. The three sites of the program admitted their first students in September 1994. Whether a 6-month diploma exit would form a part of the proposal remained uncertain even though the UNBC was not actually promoting this option (personal communication, Dr. David Fish, August 10, 1995).

Alberta

In Alberta, planning began in 1985 for the collaborative program between the University of Alberta and Red Deer College, offered in 1990-1991. A diploma exit was offered, and students who chose this option were required to complete a 23-week program following the second year of the program (University of Alberta, 1990). The University of Alberta and the four other Edmonton schools of nursing (three hospital diploma programs and one college program) extended the concept of a collaborative baccalaureate degree program already developed with Red Deer and all schools participated in a new effort to develop a 4-year integrated baccalaureate curriculum for all schools. This program began in the fall of 1991, and the 6-month diploma exit was offered only at Grant MacEwan College following 2 years at any of the program sites offering the first 2 years of the 4-year program. The Alberta government in 1994 decided to close hospital diploma schools of nursing and cut back the size of their operations by 50%, meaning that student placements and resources of the three Edmonton hospital collaborative sites were transferred to the University of Alberta and Grant MacEwan College in April, 1995. The fact that the curriculum at all schools had been the same collaborative curriculum offered by all schools meant a smoother transition than otherwise would have been the case.

In Calgary, government approval of the Conjoint Program between the University of Calgary Faculty of Nursing and the two diploma schools of nursing (Department of Nursing at Mount Royal College and the School of Nursing at Foothills Hospital) allowed the program to be implemented in September, 1993. The Alberta government's decision to close hospital-based schools of nursing meant that the remaining nursing education resources of the Foothills Hospital School of Nursing were transferred to the University of Calgary and Mount Royal College.

Saskatchewan and Manitoba

In Saskatchewan, a Nursing Education Coalition of the College of Nursing at the University of Saskatchewan and the diploma programs at Kelsey (Saskatoon) and Wascana (Regina) Institutes was established to develop a new nursing degree program in the spring of 1994 and plans for a proposed program were to be sent to the University of Saskatchewan, the Saskatchewan Institute of Applied Arts and Technology (SIAST), and the Saskatchewan Registered Nurses Association for approval by the fall of 1995. The program proposal is for a 4-year program with a diploma exit at the end of the third year and is projected as beginning to accept students in the fall of 1996. In the meantime, diploma programs at Kelsey and Wascana Institutes would continue to operate (Saskatchewan Registered Nurses Association, 1994, p. 10).

The collaborative initiative implemented in Manitoba in 1991 developed into a consolidated effort by 1994. The 4-year baccalaureate degree program in nursing that developed was offered at the University of Manitoba and, beginning in 1991, at the Manitoba Health Sciences Centre. At the latter site and at the St. Boniface site, which joined the collaboration in 1992, 1 year of the program was added per year until all 4 years were offered. As the initiative was implemented and in view of the changing health-care environment and health-care reform, the participants developed a consolidated arrangement so that blended teaching teams at the various sites were used to avoid duplication of effort (personal communication, I. Bramadat, September 2, 1994). At the University of Brandon, where a 2-year post-RN degree program had been offered, the university, Brandon General Hospital, and the Grace Hospital in Winnipeg collaborated to offer a 4-year degree program in nursing at these sites.

Ontario

In the provinces of Ontario, Quebec, and Saskatchewan, all hospital-based diploma schools of nursing were transferred to the colleges pursuant to provincial government decisions in the 1960s and 1970s. In Ontario, nine university nursing programs and 23 diploma programs in the colleges make planning for baccalaureate entry-to-practice perhaps more complex than in some of the other provinces. However, two proposals for restructuring basic nursing education to ensure that students have the opportunity to earn a baccalaureate degree in initial programs of nursing education were funded by the Ontario government (CNA, winter 1992-1993a). The first project involved two universities and two community colleges. In the collaborative effort of Laurentian University and Cambrian College, the new 4-year collaborative program was planned to commence in the fall of 1996. At the time of writing, the participants had not decided whether to offer a diploma exit (personal communication, C. Vanderlee, September 1, 1994). The University of Western Ontario and Fanshawe College collaborated to develop a program that had yet to be approved by the senate of the University at the time of writing. In this cooperative effort a 4-year program with a common curriculum at both sites was planned. However, the participants had not decided whether to offer a diploma exit at the time of writing (personal communication, L. Bramwell, September 1, 1994). When the joint working groups at the Ontario institutions began their work, the Ministry of Health "decreed that a consortium be formed to formulate 'a coherent and consistent province-wide approach,' which provides for 'accessibility and equity' without threat to the diploma exit" (Canadian Nurses Association, winter 1992-1993, p. 1).

In the other project funded by the Ontario government, Queen's University collaborated with 4-college nursing programs—St. Lawrence College-St. Laurent in Kingston, Brockville, Cornwall, and Loyalist College. In this project, still at an early stage of development, a committee representing the five institutions was meeting and working on a collaborative curriculum as well as on transfer of credits. Although the committee had not yet selected a model, the resulting program was expected to have a common curriculum, be 4 years in length, and offer a diploma exit (personal communication, S. Estabrooks, August 31, 1994). These initiatives undoubtedly will lead to further developments in Ontario.

Quebec

In Quebec, the CEGEP system of preparation allows for 2 years of preparation in the college system, followed by 3 years at the university level leading to a degree in nursing. The colleges also offer diploma programs in nursing for those not planning to take a degree in nursing.

In 1993, a study by an organization of nursing administrators in Quebec (l'Association des directeurs et responsables des soins infirmiers du Québec) stimulated discussion of the need for nurses prepared at the baccalaureate level. In the report of their study of the future needs for nurses in health care, it was concluded that the nurse of the future should be prepared in a university and that those entering the practice of nursing should hold a baccalaureate degree in nursing.[*] It is likely that the debate stimulated by this influential group of nursing administrators will stimulate considerable discussion and reflection about the development of collaborative baccalaureate programs between the CEGEP programs and the universities (l'Association des directeurs et responsables des soins infirmier du Québec, 1993, p. 1). More attempts to improve standards of nursing education are likely and undoubtedly will be successful when a consensus is reached on an appropriate course of action by nurses at all levels of the profession.

Atlantic Provinces

In the east, the province of Prince Edward Island became the first to implement the entry-to-practice position in 1988, with the closure of the only diploma school of nursing in that province and the simultaneous establishment of a baccalaureate degree program at the University of Prince Edward Island. Efforts are underway in Newfoundland, Nova Scotia, and New Brunswick to develop collaborative baccalaureate programs. The Nurse Educators Interest Group of the New Brunswick Association of Registered Nurses has led discussions on the collaboration between the five diploma and two university programs in nursing. The diploma schools of nursing had not been officially closed as of the time of writing (personal communication, N. Wiggins, September 1, 1994), even though New Brunswick's Premier

---

[*]Translation from the original French, which is: "L'infirmière de l'avenir devra à l'université. L'accès à la profession d'infirmière devra passer par l'acquisition d'un baccalauréat de base en sciences infirmières.

McKenna has been the only provincial premier to publicly support baccalaureate entry-to-practice. In Nova Scotia, Dalhousie University and two diploma programs have collaborated (CNA, September, 1992). The three institutions are to launch a program in the fall of 1995, when the two diploma programs (Victoria General Hospital—Camp Hill Medical Complex and Yarmouth Regional Hospital School of Nursing) will close. The three sites planned one curriculum with no diploma exit, and in which all nursing students are to be registered at Dalhousie University (personal communication, W. Dundas, September 1, 1994). Meanwhile in Newfoundland, Memorial University and four diploma schools of nursing have planned a degree program in nursing, also without a diploma exit. The diploma schools included the General Hospital, the Salvation Army Grace General Hospital, St. Clare's Mercy Hospital, and Western Memorial Regional Hospital (CNA, Winter 1992-1993b).

■ Graduate Education in Nursing

Master's Degree Programs in Nursing Flourish

Since the first master's degree program in nursing was established at the University of Western Ontario in 1959, graduate education at the master's level has grown to include 16 master's programs in nursing, with three established in the 1960s (McGill University, 1961; University of Montreal, 1965; and University of British Columbia, 1968); four in the 1970s (University of Toronto, 1970; University of Alberta, 1975; Dalhousie University, 1975; and University of Manitoba, 1979); three in the 1980s (University of Calgary, 1981; Memorial University of Newfoundland, 1982; and University of Saskatchewan, 1986); and five in the 1990s (Laval University, 1991; University of Ottawa, 1993; Queen's University, 1994; University of Windsor, 1994; and McMaster University, 1994) (Ross Kerr, 1996). The University of Ottawa program was the first master's program in nursing to be offered as a bilingual program in English and French.

Nurses prepared as clinical specialists who can serve as expert practitioners and teachers have been needed for some time. In Ontario, programs currently are being implemented to prepare nurse practitioners at the post-baccalaureate level. Achieving the entry-to-practice goal depends on the accessibility and availability of graduate work in nursing. Therefore graduate programs strong in clinical and research preparation are key elements in expanding the ranks of well-prepared clinical nurse specialists in acute care agencies, community-health agencies, and faculties of nursing. The development and expansion of university programs in nursing at the baccalaureate level cannot be accomplished without the infusion of considerable numbers of faculty members prepared at the master's and doctoral levels.

A primary issue in the 36 years since the first master's degree programs in nursing were established has been accessibility of programs, both geographically and in program capacity. Master's programs have been established in most regions of the country. However, whether existing master's programs have sufficient capacity is a matter of debate. The Canadian Nurses Association has stated that "the rate of growth in admissions (to master's programs in nursing) has not kept pace with the growth in applications" (Canadian Nurses Association, Winter 1992-1993, p. 2). While applications to master's programs went up 50% between 1987 and 1991, admissions rose only 24%. While there were 12 master's programs for 262,288 registered nurses in Canada employed in nursing in 1991, there were 16 master's programs in social work for 48,591 social workers (Canadian Nurses Association, Winter 1992-1993, p. 2). With interactive videoconference technology becoming more available and affordable, requests for delivery of master's programs in nursing at a distance confirm the need for this level of education in nursing across a wider geographic area.

Program quality has been high, and programs have been characterized by rigorous research preparation, because until 1991 no doctoral programs in nursing were available in Canada for the preparation of nursing researchers. A strong clinical base in master's degree programs was slow to develop, because the early programs offered only functional specialization in nursing education and nursing administration. Clinical concentration in areas of interest has become an important goal in programs, and virtually all programs seek to prepare graduates for an advanced level of nursing practice.

The thesis component of master's degree programs has been controversial. In the United States, master's degree programs in nursing eliminated the thesis requirement as doctoral programs in nursing increased in number and accessibility, thus allowing nursing researchers to be prepared at the doctoral level. In Canada since the 1980s, some programs have been established without the option to complete a thesis, and others have altered their requirements to allow clinical concentration as an alternative to a focus on research. This undoubtedly has been influenced both by the pattern of most programs in the United States and by the establishment of doctoral programs in Canada.

The Inception of Doctoral Programs in Nursing

The quest to establish a doctoral program in nursing in Canada gained momentum in 1978 when the CNA sponsored a national Seminar on Doctoral Preparation for Canadian Nurses and published the proceedings (Zilm, Larose, and Stinson, 1979). As a result of this seminar, the CNA, the Canadian Nurses Foundation (CNF), and the Canadian Association of University Schools of Nursing (CAUSN) proposed "Operation Bootstrap" and sought $5.2 million from the W.K. Kellogg Foundation. Its purpose was to obtain establishment grants for the PhD in Nursing programs, two nursing research consortia, emergency fellowships for doctoral preparation, and funding for communicating nursing research and maintaining an inventory of nurses with doctoral preparation. Although funding was not obtained, the plans for the infrastructure to support doctoral programs provided a model that helped nursing education administrators to plan for the development of programs in universities where such programs were needed.

The admission of students to the first fully funded doctoral program in nursing in Canada, in January of 1991 at the University of Alberta, was a milestone for the nursing profession in Canada, because efforts to fund doctoral programs had fallen on deaf ears until then. A second doctoral program in nursing was funded at the University of British Columbia in September, 1991, and two additional programs began in the fall of 1993 at the University of Toronto and jointly at McGill University and l'université de Montréal. In the fall of 1994, McMaster University launched a fifth program. A number of special case students had been admitted to McGill University and the University of Alberta before bona fide doctoral programs were funded, and the first student to receive a PhD in Nursing from a Canadian university was a special case student from McGill who graduated in the fall of 1990. The first PhD in nursing in a fully funded program was awarded at the University of Alberta in 1992.

Issues in doctoral education in nursing include the quality and accessibility of programs. Research funds and productivity have increased sharply in university schools and faculties of nursing that developed graduate programs over the past 2 decades. This has occurred gradually as a result of an increasing number of nurses with preparation in research and the greater availability of funding for nursing research investigations. Faculties must have a commitment to research if outstanding graduate programs in nursing are to be developed, and research-granting agencies must target nursing as a discipline for funding. The National Health Research and Development Program of Health Canada has funded nursing research over a considerable period of time. In 1994, the Medical Research Council (MRC) announced that it was broadening its mandate from medical research exclusively to encompass health research. The MRC now funds a broader range of health disciplines that fall within its mandate.

■ Distance Education in Nursing

The revolution in communications technology and the information superhighway potentially can increase and enhance all activities and services that involve communication between individuals or groups. The new generation of equipment capable of transferring compressed video data is affordable enough to bring videoconferencing through telephone lines to the doorstep of higher education. The question is no longer whether postsecondary institutions employing traditional modes of instruction will find uses for the new technology, but whether postsecondary institutions as we know them will survive in their present form. No longer can institutions of higher learning assume that all students can physically be present in the classroom. Likewise, no longer can some universities and colleges pursue solely traditional methods of teaching while newer institutions concentrate on distance applications. Consumer demand and resulting choices will ensure that no institution can afford to ignore the new communications technology for teaching and learning.

Students can benefit greatly from the technological revolution beginning in higher education. Traditional methods of teaching will be enriched by the transition to a more interactive process in which students are challenged to be active participants. Increasing competition among institutions to attract the most capable students may lead to greater incorporation of nontraditional methods into mainstream courses and programs at the undergraduate and graduate levels. Higher proportions of mature students, students also engaged in full-time employment, and those from minority ethnic and cultural backgrounds also will help to increase the acceptance of nontraditional approaches and the geographic dispersion of students in courses and programs. University libraries are at the leading edge of the technological revolution, as they convert their indexes into large databases accessible to the university community through computers and modems both on campus and at distant locations.

Major universities will be more likely to achieve the goal of baccalaureate entry-to-practice by offering programs to students in more geographic locations than the settings in which the major university campuses are located. In this instance, a primary professional goal could be achieved through the use of technology. This technology is being applied to graduate education in nursing and is likely to increase in the future. More nurses who are prepared to engage in advanced nursing practice in a variety of settings are urgently needed, and distance methods provide the means of delivering programs to groups of students in diverse locations who both desire and need this preparation.

Nursing education has been at the forefront of the information revolution, developing post-RN degree programs available at a distance long before courses were available through distance technology in other faculties and university departments. Leaders in distance education in Canada have been Athabasca University, the University of Alberta, the University of Ottawa, and the University of Victoria. Others that more recently began offering their degrees or degree courses through distance technology in the west include the University of Saskatchewan and the University of British Columbia. In Ontario, Laurentian University began offering a post-RN baccalaureate degree in nursing through distance methods in 1987. In the east, Dalhousie University has offered courses in outpost nursing through distance methods, Memorial University has offered their post-RN courses by distance through a cooperative brokering arrangement with Athabasca University in Alberta, and St. Francis Xavier has offered a small distance program since 1989. Distance programs in nursing degree programs initially offered post-RN baccalaureate programs, which were shorter and encompassed fewer nursing courses than their basic degree-program counterparts. As universities offering degree programs and colleges throughout the regions and provinces develop collaborative arrangements, the value of distance technology becomes apparent. This specialized equipment has become more available and affordable, allowing universities to offer courses themselves or in cooperation with college faculty as location becomes less of a problem. The "campus without walls" becomes a reality as interactive videoconferencing technology is incorporated into "traditional" basic integrated degree programs in nursing in universities.

As undergraduate programs become more available at a distance, schools are attempting to extend such arrangements to prospective graduate students at the master's and doctoral levels who live at a distance from universities. Some universities have offered their programs through distance technology for some time. The universities of Alberta and Calgary experimented with fully interactive videoconferencing technology and offered selected nursing courses at the master's level in academic sessions during 1979-1980, 1980-1981, and 1981-1982. After further experiments in undergraduate programming through teleconferencing technology, a pilot project offered an entire master's degree program to a group of students situated in Red Deer, Alberta in 1992. The success of this program and the availability of resources to offer courses and entire programs at a distance will determine the type of graduate degree programs to be offered at a distance by the University of Alberta.

■ Preparation for Specialty Practice

The growth in the knowledge base in nursing over the past 3 decades has produced more areas of specialization in nursing. The increased need for specialized preparation has created new demands for basic nursing education and for the health-care agencies in which nursing is practised. The tremendous growth in the knowledge base in nursing has challenged educators to determine what is core subject matter and should be taught in basic programs and what is specialized subject matter beyond the scope of the basic program. Such dilemmas become more difficult as nursing knowledge grows rapidly while the time available for courses is finite.

Concerns over safe practice have led health-care institutions, colleges, and universities to offer a variety of specialized courses. In the past, health-care agencies often offered courses on a full-time apprenticeship basis. This practice ensured that particular departments had sufficient qualified staff members. In some cases, agencies subsidized the cost of operating a unit by paying the full-time registered nurse–students wages lower than standard wages for registered nurses. Because these RN students practised on the nursing units during the time they were not in class, this was advantageous for the agency. Even though tuition costs and books were included in some programs, the agency had to cover the costs of hiring instructors to teach the program. With many more educational opportunities available in nursing and other fields that did not require students to subsidize the costs of operating the service agency, agencies had a difficulty attracting students to such courses. In addition, to ensure that staff have the knowledge and skills to function in specialty areas, some agencies have developed sophisticated orientation programs. What constitutes orientation and what constitutes specialty education for which an institution of higher learning should take responsibility remains an issue. Nursing service administrators thus have tended to promote specialty programs in educational institutions, and service agencies have collaborated in the development of a number of specialty courses.

The CNA now determines standards for specialty courses taken for certification in nursing specialties. Recognizing that certification is a voluntary process requiring periodic updating, the CNA has described the three purposes of a certification mechanism as: "(1) to provide an opportunity for practitioners to validate their expertise in a specialty; (2) to promote high standards of nursing practice in order to provide quality nursing care to the people of Canada; and (3) to identify, through a recognized credential, those nurses who have met the specialty standards" (CNA, 1986, p. 2). To be designated a specialty for certification, a group must meet seven criteria: "(has) established standards, addresses recurrent phenomena in practice, role description for practitioners (is) available, (is) supported by literature, education and research, provides care for a defined population, has identified the number and distribution of nurses practising in the specialty, and has the human resources available to support the certification process" (personal communication, L. A. Patry, October 3, 1994). The CNA certification process also requires a certification examination that is continuously updated. The CNA uses the principle of cost recovery to determine the costs of the process. Nurses applying for certification in a specialty must meet several criteria to be eligible to write the examinations. These include current active registration in a province or territory, experiential background in the field of specialty, and a satisfactory performance record. The CNA distinguishes between the nurse who successfully completes the certification process in a specialty and the clinical nurse specialist who is prepared at the master's degree level in nursing (CNA, 1986).

Several universities have collaborated to develop specialty programs that grant credit toward a baccalaureate degree in nursing. At first, most of these credits were applied to post-RN baccalaureate programs. Recently, some have been applied to basic programs. However, baccalaureate programs limit the time that can be spent in specialty areas, because the student first must have a good general knowledge in nursing. When specialty courses are available at the baccalaureate level, they tend to be offered as senior clinical courses in the third or fourth year of the program. However, because nursing has entered the age of specialization, health care knowledge is increasingly complex, and nurses in highly technical areas require extensive knowledge and excellent clinical judgement, educational institutions must incorporate some specialty education within their undergraduate degree programs.

■ Monitoring Standards in Nursing Education

All types of educational programs must have standards to promote quality and ensure that at least minimal requirements are met. Standards range from minimal to ideal, depending on their purpose. Nursing has two basic mechanisms for monitoring educational programs: approval and accreditation. Approval is a process that determines an educational institution's competence to prepare practitioners for entry to nursing practice, that is, approval grants permission to operate a nursing program. The standards set by the monitoring body usually are minimal, whereas the standards established for accreditation of programs are intended to promote quality.

Approval is a mandatory process, and minimal standards are established by a body authorized by provincial legislation, or regulations pursuant to that legislation. On the other hand, accreditation is voluntary, is national in scope and measures institutions against criteria established by the accrediting body to promote quality. Accreditation of educational programs exists in many professions, but approval and monitoring of programs are unique to nursing. No other profession is governed by legislation that regulates the conduct of educational programs; however, nursing is the only profession that does not require university-level preparation for entry to practice. Because diploma-level education continues in nursing, standards can vary widely; thus the monitoring mechanism of approval is essential.

The purpose of any credentialing mechanism is to protect the public and ensure accountability to consumers. In nursing education programs, the consumers are the students, although patients or clients are the ultimate consumers of the services provided by nursing students and by graduates of nursing programs. Because any system of credentialing also benefits the institutions or individuals who are credentialed, the credentialing mechanism needs a system of checks and balances to ensure that the public is protected. In both approval and accreditation, standards provide the checks and balances that ensure that the practitioners prepared in nursing education programs are competent to enter the practice of professional nursing.

Approval

In Canada, constitutional responsibility for education and health care rests with the provinces. Consequently, each province defines the policies and mechanisms for monitoring nursing education standards. This responsibility is delineated in legislation that regulates the conduct of educational programs, whether conducted in universities, colleges, or hospital schools of nursing. In all provinces except Alberta, Ontario, and Quebec, the provincial nursing association assumes the responsibility for defining and monitoring standards in nursing education. In Alberta, this responsibility is delegated to the Universities' Coordinating Council, which has responsibility for defining and monitoring standards for all postsecondary education in the province. In Ontario, the College of Nurses of Ontario (CNO) fulfils the registration and discipline functions for registered nurses and registered nursing assistants. In Quebec, all postsecondary education, including nursing programs, is governed by the Ministry of Higher Education and Science. There has been no mechanism for approval of nursing programs; however, a mechanism for approval is being developed for the diploma programs in Quebec, and the university nursing programs are subject to the approval process required of all educational programs in their respective universities.

Because of the number and variety of nursing education programs, one can expect considerable differences in the systems for regulation and monitoring. The standards for nursing education programs in each province cover such areas as administration, organization, philosophy and objectives, faculty, students, curriculum, educational resources and facilities, records, reports, and evaluation. These standards must be defined by well-prepared, competent nurses and ideally this regulatory mechanism falls under the professional nursing association. Standards must be defined broadly enough to allow programs to have creative approaches while maintaining basic accountability to the public and to the consumers of nursing education, the students. Approval must be obtained to establish a new program in nursing, and monitoring for continued approval occurs at 5-year intervals. Approval must also be obtained to eliminate a nursing program. In the approval process, the nursing program submits a report, then reviewers designated by the authorized body visit the program. These individuals normally are qualified registered nurses who report their recommendations to the appropriate body. In most provinces, nursing education programs in universities are required to meet the standards defined by the university according to an act governing the universities; these programs usually are not required to participate in the approval process defined for the diploma programs.

Accreditation

Accreditation of educational programs is a voluntary process designed to promote quality. Canada had no system for accreditation of nursing education programs until 1986, when the Canadian Association of University Schools of Nursing (CAUSN) established such a program after devoting 12 years to its development. A major impetus for the program was that nursing was one of the few health sciences educational programs that did not have a system for accreditation. Further impetus came from the university nursing programs in Ontario and Quebec, which needed an approval process to satisfy the governmental agency responsible for registration or licensure of registered nurses.

Criteria were delineated by CAUSN's Committee on Accreditation to use as a basis for evaluating the programs: (1) *relevance* to trends in society that influence health needs of the community, (2) *accountability*, or the extent to which the program teaches students that the primary responsibility in nursing is to the client, (3) *relatedness*, or the extent to which parts of the program support and build on other parts, and (4) *uniqueness*, or the extent to which a program capitalizes on the resources within its particular setting. Several university nursing programs across Canada served as test sites in developing standards and instruments over the 12 years before the CAUSN Council approved the accreditation program for implementation.

Because accreditation is a voluntary process, university nursing programs choose whether and when to seek accreditation. These decisions are influenced by many factors, including the availability of funds to participate and the need to use it as an option to the program approval process required in some provinces. Provinces where the latter is a factor include Ontario, Quebec, and Nova Scotia. CAUSN implements its accreditation function through a Board of Accreditation, which includes six members appointed by the CAUSN Council who function within the policies and guidelines established by the association. By 1993, 12 of the university nursing programs were reviewed and accredited for either a 3-year or 7-year period. Ten other schools are scheduled for review over the next 5 years, of which five are seeking accreditation. As expected, most of the programs seeking accreditation initially were in the three provinces in which accreditation is an option to the program approval process.

CAUSN employs accreditation for two major purposes: to promote quality in nursing education and to recognize programs that have met specific standards. To date there is no stated means of providing information about the accreditation status of schools to prospective students, to guidance counsellors, or to nurses interested in earning a baccalaureate degree in nursing. Perhaps this will be done in the future, but, to be useful, information about denial of accreditation would have to be placed in the public domain as well as information about accredited programs.

The major issue pertaining to the CAUSN accreditation program is whether 30 university nursing education units in Canada can support such a program with annual membership fees plus a special accreditation fee. The range of annual membership fees is $3000 for 1 to 99 full-time equivalent (FTE) students; $3500 for 100 to 199; $4000 for 200 to 299; $4500 for 300 to 399; $5000 for 400 to 499; and $5500 for more than 500 (CAUSN Council, 1989). Yet to be determined is whether the annual income generated by this fee structure, plus the $5000 accreditation fee paid by universities seeking accreditation, and the $500 annual accreditation program fee assessed the universities not seeking accreditation in that year will be enough to support all CAUSN programs.

Another issue of accreditation is the faculty time required by the process. This includes time required by the self-study process, which may be extended over a year, and the time required for faculty to serve as visitors to other schools and as review board members. This takes time from research, which is vitally important in the academic community and to advancement of nursing knowledge and improvement of nursing practice. If accreditation criteria do not emphasize and require research, the process of accreditation may not help to promote research as an integral part of the faculty role. Thomas, Arseneault, Bouchard, Côté, and Stanton (1992) reported that the schools that completed the evaluation tools designed to assess the accreditation process reported that "the self-study process was found to be very time-consuming . . . even though it increased awareness and stimulated discussion about the programme among faculty and students" (p. 41). Thomas and Arseneault (1992) concur that the self-study is time-consuming and increases faculty workload and stress but also fosters self-development and reinforces issues already recognized. Thus the goal of accreditation, to promote quality, depends on the extent to which the process influences not only standards of education, but also research productivity designed to improve nursing practice.

■ The Future of Nursing Education

The broad scope of this chapter attests to the tremendous range of issues in nursing education. Health-care reform is creating exciting opportunities for the profession as all services are restructured at a rapid rate. As more health services are offered in the community, direct access to nursing services probably will be permitted in at least some regions of the country. As patterns of practice undergo such fundamental change, nursing education at the baccalaureate, master's, and doctoral levels will need to change as well to prepare practitioners for practice in the future. Monitoring, approval, and accreditation of programs must reflect the changes in the profession and in the educational programs. Distance methods will be used broadly in nursing education to offer the new collaborative undergraduate programs in nursing between institutions and to remote groups of students. Distance technology also will be used much more widely in the future in graduate nursing education. The trend toward specialization in nursing likely will continue. The continued growth in nursing knowledge means that nurses in various specialties need appropriate educational support. In this climate of change, the opportunities for the profession in the future are limitless. The strong leadership that always has characterized the profession likely will continue to lead the development of nursing education systems that prepare practitioners to meet the needs of health-care consumers of the future.

■ REFERENCES

Alberta Association of Registered Nurses. (1976). *Response to the Alberta Task Force on Nursing Education.* Edmonton, Alberta: the Association.

Alberta Task Force on Nursing Education. (1975). *Report of the Alberta Task Force on Nursing Education.* Edmonton, Alberta: the task force.

Canadian Association of University Schools of Nursing. Minutes of council meeting of November 17, 1989.

Canadian Nurses Association. (1982). *Entry to the practice of nursing: A background paper.* Ottawa: the Association.

Canadian Nurses Association. (1986). *CNA's certification program: An information booklet.* Ottawa: the Association.

Canadian Nurses Association. (September 1991a). NB for BN: Province joins nurses' call for degree. *Edufacts, 1*(2), 1.

Canadian Nurses Association. (September 1991b). Manitoba phasing out two programs: Joint program begins. *Edufacts, 1*(2), 1, 4.

Canadian Nurses Association. (June 1992). Collaboration among all Saskatchewan nursing schools. *Edufacts, 2*(2), 4.

Canadian Nurses Association. (September 1992). New BN education—Nova Scotia style: Three nursing schools collaborate to offer a baccalaureate program. *Edufacts, 2*(3), 1.

Canadian Nurses Association. (Summer 1993a). Calgary conjoint nursing program: A dream realized. *Edufacts, 3*(2), 1.

Canadian Nurses Association. (Winter 1992-1993a). Ontario edging closer to entry to practice? *Edufacts, 2*(4), 1, 3.

Canadian Nurses Association. (Winter 1992-1993b). Joint funding for Newfoundland collaboration. *Edufacts, 2*(4), 4.

L'Association des directeurs et responsables des soins infirmiers du Québec. (1993). "L'évolution des soins infirmiers au Qeébec: pour une dynamique d'amélioration continue." Quebec: the Association.

Lord, A.R. (1952). *Report of the evaluation of the Metropolitan School of Nursing, Windsor, Ontario.* Ottawa: Canadian Nurses Association.

Nurses Association of New Brunswick (1992). *Annual Reports 1991-1992.* Fredericton, New Brunswick: the Association.

Ross Kerr, J. (1996) The growth of graduate education in nursing. In J. Ross Kerr and J. MacPhail (Eds.), *Canadian nursing: Issues and perspectives.* Toronto: Mosby–Year Book.

Saskatchewan Registered Nurses Association. (August 1994). Nursing Education Coalition (NEC) update. *ConceRN*, p. 10.

Thomas, B., Arseneault, A., Bouchard, J., Coté, E. & Stanton, S. (1992). Accreditation of university nursing programmes in Canada. *Canadian Journal of Nursing Research, 24*(2), 33-48.

Thomas, B., & Arseneault, A. (1992). Organizing your schools for accreditation. *Canadian Journal of Nursing Research, 24*(2), 58-59.

University of Alberta. (1990) Collaborative nursing program with Red Deer College approved. *Folio*, January 18, p.3.

Zilm, G., Larose, O., & Stinson, S. (1979). *Proceedings of the Kellogg National Seminar on Doctoral Education for Canadian Nurses.* Ottawa: Canadian Nurses Association.

■ Index